Contents

Publisher's Preface
by Stanley Moss

In 1960 Laurence Lieberman, accustomed to the warm south of California, offered a good job at Reed College in the moral north of Oregon and a job at the University of the Virgin Islands at St. Thomas, because of his ache for "adventure" chose St. Thomas, where he stayed four years, returning every year for the next twenty. His need for "adventure" perhaps synonymous with Goethe's "flight into elsewhere." Adventure also meant to Lieberman not being chained to the oars and galleys of MFA teaching programs. The Caribbean was, of course, full of the beauty of new, invisible music heard by Alexander Hamilton, created in part by African slaves, "freed" by the British in 1837—the natural beauty, music, smells, tastes, etc. were and still are experienced by visitors and resident workers, some truly free, others still indentured by the twentieth and twenty-first centuries' protocols, politics and other refinements. Still others, with their beautiful post-African, post English, French, Dutch, and Spanish empire accents, have left the tourist paradise for northern republics. Other English-language writers who immediately come to mind who have used Caribbean island and post-island life as a launching site are Derek Walcott, V. S. Naipaul, Mark Strand, and F. T. Prince. I have not forgotten the Cubans and, if one gets blown from the islands off course to the mainland far enough, Neruda and the other Latins: some of Lieberman's immortals.

Adventure to Laurence Lieberman was hunting for and finding poetry and a new way of life. This book of books and occasional poems is full of wonder-filled tales married by book covers, a ship's log of plain talk, metaphors and allegories. Lieberman really "swims with the immortals." He often does not replace "telling" with "showing," as Eliot and Pound called for.

This "book" joins four parts/acts (five acts being the basic structure of tragedy), begins with a big bang!—an homage to Marianne Moore—that flows on a pastoral-tragical river of syllable-counted lines, which shows us not only what years are, but what can come of such devotion, that also always sings in praise of language. Throughout this book there's also the good ghost, I mean troll, of Dylan Thomas, poems that sail in the strait of the imagination, in the Caribbean and the North Sea off the coast of Wales, at Laugharne and Swansea and St. Kitts—uncharted waters.

In manuscript, some Lieberman pages assumed that I, the reader, knew the characters—their occupations, religious practices, their home address, their geography and geology—when I did not have the pleasure or pain of their acquaintance. Therefore I asked Lieberman to write brief "The Poet on the Poem" essays, rather than provide academic footnotes. ("The Poet on the Poem," for which the angel of life and death, Steve Berg, *American Poetry Review* editor and founder, holds the patent.) Lieberman's "The Poet on the Poem" for "Opera" is not criticism but a beautiful and moving prose poem, swimming among a pod of whales. I notice Lieberman is not tempted to supply any technical information, no defense or celebration of his own style. Never a tourist, Lieberman enters Caribbean life as a wandering Jew.

Lieberman's great poem "Transvestite" is his almost best. It is without a "The Poet on the Poem" essay. I've tried to find a section of the poem I could quote, but to do so would have the vulgarity of amputation—it would not be a Venus without arms, it would be a Venus without arms and head—so I here quote the whole of it:

TRANSVESTITE

I must undo my robes of the air,
    untie my earth

THE DIVEMASTER:
SWIMMING WITH
THE IMMORTALS

Laurence Lieberman

Sheep Meadow Press
Rhinebeck, NY

Designed and typeset by The Sheep Meadow Press
Distributed by The University Press of New England

Cover Image: Detail of *Cinque Sensi* by Angelo Caroselli

Library of Congress Cataloging-in-Publication Data

Lieberman, Laurence.
  [Poetry. Selections]
  The divemaster : swimming with the immortals / Laurence
Lieberman.
      pages cm
  ISBN 978-1-937679-52-1 (alk. paper)
  I. Title.
  PS3562.I43A6 2015
  811'.54--dc23

                              2015024431

All inquiries and permission requests should be addressed to the
publisher:

The Sheep Meadow Press
PO Box 84
Rhinebeck, NY 12514

cloak
of foreignness, step out of my fear-being,
          ease into my sea
     skin
of a fish. I must enter my salt-self,
          drawing the smooth
     current
about me like heavenly drapes.
          A brainy stranger,
     I divest
crew cut and gold fillings, the silver
          ring on my wedding
finger
the water-tight wise ticker at my wrist
          proudly droning
     its one
secret to the wet world's deafness:
          Time's muffled
     bees' buzzing.
I must unremember my name, my birthplace,
          the number on my license
     plates,
my address, the brand of my children's
          toothpaste, the blessed
     earth-smell
of my wife's hair: to belong here
          I become a nameless
     dumb
free and easy man-thing. A presence
          infinitely deep
     blue-green,
full, rain-caressive, invites me,
          opens to one just
     opening
up, who, not now as a lame
          stranger, may
     enter.
I take in my hands all, all
          that I touch,
     and leave
no fingerprints. No signature.

John Keats spoke of negative capability: I believe this poem "Transvestite" drools with it. The poem will hang around in the company of America's great poems.

Any study of Lieberman's theology must observe that his style makes poetry out of the most ordinary, everyday matters. Readers can fall into the trap that the book is ordinary, but the reader should remember, by mischance, that the Ordinary, "in Roman Catholic and Western Christian liturgy, refers to the part of the Eucharist or of the canonical hours that is reasonably constant without regard to the date on which the service is performed." There is an otherworldliness to this book, but an otherworldliness as in Roethke's "In a Dark Time": "In a dark time, the eye begins to see." An adventure, perhaps, to come as close to God as possible. Somehow he simply stands before an almost invisible Ark of the Covenant.

On the island of St. Martin, Lieberman finds "Undying Is an Art," a song, a speaker notes in "The Poet on the Poem": "'If a man's too ill to crawl to church, we bring the church to him.' He must not lose his concert, it would be his first unhymned Sunday in 70 plus years." I misread "unhymned" as "unrhymed"—Harold Bloom and Lieberman would allow me my mistake, I think. Larry's poem "Largesse" can be read as a metaphor for his language:

> Salt Cay's the tiniest isle
>   in the chain, where most animals wander freely about—
>   donkeys, goats, sheep, horses
> may turn up anyplace. Unbranded, none wears
>   tags, but they know to whom they belong: where to drift
>   to be fed, that's proof
>   of ownership . . .

I think such poems would unbraid Marianne Moore's once braided hair. Standing on Parnassus, she'd throw off a three-cornered hat with joy and let her hair blow in the winds of Delphi.

For all those who have a special love for trees and butterflies, Lieberman's "Exodus of Butterflies" gorgeously points out their necessity. The butterfly exodus occurs because a 500-year-old tree is felled. Lieberman and I have a common requited love for trees and butterflies and other living holy things. (I don't have the email address of Jesus, but I very much doubt that he approves of the cutting down of an evergreen and calling it a Christmas tree to celebrate his name and birth).

I should give more than a passing nod to Larry's poem "White Gold": salt. Something I must avoid to stay alive, that "finicky George Washington always procured / for his soldiers to best preserve their meats," that some need to eat daily in fistfuls to stay alive. Dear reader, you old salt, give a little special attention to this beautiful poem. Adventure, like love, "calls us to the things of this world."

Larry Lieberman's masterwork is "THE ST. KITTS MONKEY FEUDS," a profound allegory that could not keep this reader from thinking of Dante's *Inferno*, when Lieberman describes an Inferno where monkeys are us, circles of unnecessary murder and cannibalism— our world—a symbolic representation of a highly unsystematized theology. Lieberman has no Aquinas or Scholastic philosopher to back him up. His poetry is undistilled from the Bible, but he is talking about us, a world distilled from his notebooks where we meet animals, monkeys and their clans slaughtered for food, profit, and revenge—not just monkeys, they're human cannibals placed in the lowest order of Hell. Lieberman's allegory (proof for much of Buddhist teaching) has one property that Dante's *Inferno* may have had for the Medieval, Renaissance, post-Renaissance and God-knows-how-long-ago reader that it never had for me, nor have I heard other Dante lovers complain about: that is, Lieberman's poem repeatedly frightens me by showing the murdering of innocents, the guilty murdering each other, infanticides. There are books that tell us planet Earth will be left to insects beyond the rainbow of God's will. I believe, this evening, Lieberman's poetry, in the end, may help the human race win.

vi

for Binnie

PART I

DIVEMASTER, SWIMMING
WITH THE IMMORTALS

(Turks & Caicos)

1.

Hah! *Another scribbler,* says Brian.
　　Every month, someone drops by
to ask questions for a book
　　　　　　or magazine piece. But only one
　　　　ever came back to show him
　　the work: Harry Ritchie,
who presents a comic
　　portrait of *Yours Truly* in his book
THE LAST FEW BITS, mapping
　　　　　　out scattered remnants of Britain's
Crown Colonies, *we still among*
　　　　　　　　the few islands snug
in the Empire's fold.
　　　　That said, he hands me just-
　　arrived volume. So I meet the touted Scuba
　　　　Baron in a chapter of text, while I
gossip with him at table, often
　　stopping to compare the original
　　　　　　with our book's Bembo
　　　　print twin . . . Now I tip my hand,
verse my mode, and he bolts
　　　　　　out of his wickerwork chair,
　　　　　a sly grin playing about his eyes
(you wouldn't think a man so amply
　　padded on waist and thighs
　　could move so fast). *Stay put,*

he says. *I'll play you a favorite*
tape of yesteryear. He scuttles
behind a pasteboard room partition—
in moments, I'm hearing the Bard
himself reciting key passages
from A CHILD'S X'MAS IN WALES.
The audio fidelity so sharp
and clear, I can hardly wait
to check out that State-of-the-Art
stereo and speaker models, following
the trail of those voice
waves into the den where—
to my astonished stare—
my host himself secretly recites
the passage into a tiny cordless
mike . . . The ghost of Thomas
flutters between us, and I bow,
shutting my eyes to study
our poet's swagger
and lullaby song lilt.
After a pause, blushing, I
whisper my apology for invading
the sanctuary and voluminous sweep
of Brian's private
library. This expert dive-master
and hotelier keeps under wraps
a secret life. His performance
tricks are the least of it.
For some years, a collector
of books, letters and rare scraps
of memorabilia from the famed literati
of his time. Age fifty-nine today,
great poets his first rage!

All the inscribed books are here,
   first editions mostly,
      often full letters appended
to them, as to a cherished pal. None
closer to Brian and his wife
         Marjorie than their grand eccentric
         neighbor of seven years
   in The Village ('62–'69):
   *Have you read her, Larry,
   at all? Marianne Moore* . . .
            They hobnobbed,
      regularly, between flats,
         she their weekly guest for dinner.
A tagalong on summer evenings,
         taking their Irish Wolf-
hounds for walks in the park
      (nearest kin, for size, to horses
they missed back at their Laramie
      Ranch), and a partner for drives
to visit gardens, arboretums, and
      (ah!) zoos. Truly, she held mellow converse
         with the caged Cheetah,
   polar bear, grizzly, more strainlessly
than with most fellow humans.
            It was no mere affectation,
      but a true affinity. Kinship. All
   instinct and magic interplay.
   An audible code of squeaks
   and counter-trills on both sides.
   A two-way merging. Suppose aboriginal
      tribes trying to find
a common ground with no language
         crossovers between them . . .

But now he's
  whisking me, volume by mint
volume, through the whole shelf of Marianne Moore's
  first editions, hand-
scripted letters tucked in all the covers or front pages, and he's
  recounting highlights of her many great
readings that he attended—the best, perhaps, those held
  at Ninety-Second-Street
Y in Manhattan. Next he shows me a prize catch. She'd gladly blessed him

    with scrawled
  notes she hurriedly penned
to herself prior to her last Y reading! And he found
  himself delighting
in many other lordly events at the Y, such as Moshe Dayan's
  final eloquent speech on behalf of United
Jewish Appeal. Brian—by his winningly modest awe—
  procured the Israeli
General's prep notes, as well. Though Miss Moore would remain his first

    love, he made
  a charmed round of visits
(*pilgrimages*, he calls his forays in search of rare
  books and letters),
near and far, to enhance his collection. Becoming a neighbor
  of Tennessee Williams in Key West one summer,
he garnered signed copies of all his plays and books.
  Visiting Eugene O'neill's
homes, he found rare documents to supplement the signed books and letter

collection
    he'd acquired with the help—
  beyond measure—of O'neill's friend Edna St. Vincent
    Millay in The Village.
  His scouting trips, hunts for literary gems, were fittingly
    capped—he recalls—by visits to the aging
  Robert Frost at his cabin retreat in Wermont. Brian's
    single biggest challenge:
sweet-talking the New England Laureate to inscribe all editions of both

    old and new
    books, which he carried with him
  to the Bard in his convertible Studebaker's trunk,
    but needed to seduce
  Frost to sell him the two earliest British firsts to complete
    his cycle. He worked the charm by reciting
  whole texts of seven of the poet's long poems from
    memory, without a slip.
The windup, his brave imitations of Frost's own voice heard on old tapes:

    his guttural
    chanting of *The Witch of Coös*
  and *The Death of the Hired Man.* Then, at the stunned
    listener's request,
  saying them again in his own personal voice register, free
    of all parody or simulation. He passed
  the test—and won the coveted volumes, inscribed
    in high form . . . Alas,
this very month, he finds that he must part with the whole Eugene O'Neill

    garnering of
    pricey letters and documents,
  for sale to Swanns to cover some pressing debts. Yes,

he hates to compromise
his sweat-inveigled treasures for money, never his intention
at the start of his journey. He was building
an archive. A pure spirit-buoying cache of scholarly
jewels. His sole wish,
to make of his home library a rare book surprise to share with few choice

friends, or
guests. How he loathes being
pressed to a crux of *sellout*! Enough said about *perils*
of lucre, he drifts
back to nostalgic high moments of his best planned or chance
meetings with *Olympians of the Pen*. And for all
those gamy happenstance joustings with arch Tennessee
in the Florida Keys,
good anecdotes though they make, no single milestone occasion can rival

the historic
hour when he drove Marianne
Moore to her appointed moment of joining the annals
of Baseball's Hall
of Fame. The one truest marriage of baseball and *Our Age's*
poetry. Her bony arm curled around his fleshy
forearm (he can still feel the featherweight gossamer
pull of her slim mass
of person), such pride he took in escorting her into the Yankee Stadium

grandstand, her
tricorne hat pinned securely
to her hair-bob, so sharp its three points a possible
weapon if you stood
too close, and hovered near her like a safety net, without
daring to reach out to graze her unless she

were surely falling out of control—as she executed
    that perfect overhand
pitch, while she hurled out to the field the inaugural ball of the season.

THE POET ON THE POEM

"Divemaster: Swimming with the Immortals"

I spent a full day in Providenciales, the capitol city of the Turks and Caicos. Swarms of tourists were all about. We made brief stops at a couple of uninhabited isles. But my arrival at near-deserted Salt Cay was saluted by Brian. I'd phoned him before sailing over, and he was excited to get advance word of my poetry books. He was pleased at the prospect of my writing a poem about him and his careers, both here and in Colorado. After teasing me with his vocal imitation of Dylan Thomas's reading, he was most cheered to learn that I shared his great passion for Marianne Moore's poetry. I was charmed by his account of the years he and his wife were neighbors and friends of Moore's in Brooklyn. He took a certain pride in mimicking her chants as she encountered animals in the local zoo.

Then, as he conducted my tour of his collection of memorabilia, Moore, Frost and Tennessee Williams all came vividly to life in his acting out key gestures and mannerisms of each literary master, one by one. No film bio of their lives could have made them as palpably alive and present for me as his spoken portrayals. I was entranced by his little vocal dramas— the actual breath and heat of those "immortals" seemed to waft into my life space. So close to the waters below the deck where I stood, their figures were swimming about me. In my fantasy we did a water dance… Later, Brian treated me to a long winding trip from one corner of the island to the other in his motorized golf cart. First we circled the Salt Cay perimeter, zigzagging in and out of every little cove and inlet. Then we crisscrossed the various small hillocks, slopes and shallow valleys of the territory. His constant free-wheeling lecture blent fascinating details of the land's geography with milestones of its history, dating back over 100 years.

CHAGALL'S RABBI:
BLACK FIRE ON WHITE FIRE

(Paramaribo, Surinam)

"And how was the Torah written? With black fire
upon white fire, as it rested on the knee of the Holy
One, blessed be He. It was fire, mixed with fire, hewn
from the fire and given by fire . . ."

(Deut. 33:2)

He will see you. Shalom—his secretary wafts my way,
    leading me through a labyrinth
        of narrow halls
           to a secluded inner office.
      She nods to a series of tall guards
  posted at every exit or transit zone. I'm O.K.
        They can let me pass. In
or out. Let me stay. If they were guard dogs, Blood-
        hounds, Dobermans, or
      German Shepherds, I swear she'd
          put my wrists
  to their snouts—one by one—to get their keen
whiffs of me . . . Next, she deposits me, self-wrapped

in the cocoon of my crossed arms, onto a swivel
      chair, to await the chief's arrival.
        The walls, mostly
          bare, contain a scattering
      of graphs and charts. Surinam's largest
company: they sell bottles, furniture, soft drinks.
        Famous *Hernandez*

Lemonade billboards abound, from roadside to oil
storage tanks. Factory
employs upwards of one-hundred-
fifty armed
security chaps. Maybe two thirds in plainclothes
garb, but easy to spot by their cramped indolence . . .

Restless, snoopy side glances . . . I'm entranced, held
afloat in the ghostly light
emitted by
the one-and-only art work
in view. The painting of a Rabbi
hugging a Torah to his breast. Dark sepias and cool
maroons, oddly becalmed
and billowing out at once—I ponder the enigma: Marc
Chagall's soft brimming
light coaxed from those dark edges,
plush Torah's
ruffled velours leaking glows from dusky color
as if blackish pigments can spit white sparks, light

glimmers eerily compounded upon the illusive voids
of light. Painter's happy genius
sends us head-
over-heels, making clowns of all
beholders, we puzzled lookers for a source
of hidden radiance. The secret insewn between layered
seams of the Torah cloak
and Tallith draped over the Rabbi's shoulders. Stays
hidden . . . Hernandez
bounds into the room on spiffy
white unstained

tennis sneakers, cheered by my total absorption
in the one portrait, wall-hung over his long desk top,

high-piled with invoice bills of lading . . . *How I love*
your Chagall Rabbi, I say. But
I'm most puzzled
by light rising from the Torah's
darkest hues. I suppose it's raw colors'
tricks upon our eyes. Ghostly sheen of the Tallith—
flung across his shoulder
bones like a shawl—bleeds into the twin boxes he hugs
to his breast like babes
wrapped in flannel blankets, infants
he comforts . . .
O it's not an original, he replies. *This print's*
merely a cheap copy—even so, hard to come by in Para-

maribo. By like scale-down and our custom, Rabbis,
here, are only half-schooled,
none yet fully
certified. You'd grade them sub-
standard, perhaps . . . Dapper, spruce,
compact, Hernandez steps back into the hall for two
minutes, parleys snappy
exchanges with three associates, thrust & parry, cocks
his head to one side
to listen, thrusts again, for it's
ever a happy
fencing bout between them: smiles mixed with stern
glances. Always, he gives of himself, but sets limits.

Couriers from other local shops, trades, seek his aid
or advice. And he breaks off
our discourse
three or four times, in mid-
sentence, to attend to their appeals.
If they stand in line, so many at once, he'll become
embarrassed . . . I offer
to leave. I mustn't impede progress. A fellow Jew, yes.
But an American
intruder—unannounced—on such
short notice,
I have no right to distract a busy man. *A truly busy*
man, says he, *is always ready to be made more busy. He's*

a weight lifter welcoming the extra pound. Ask an idle
man for his time. He'll spurn you.
He has no
cramped space to fit you in, no life
jubilance to stretch a bit more here, more
there. Stretch me, says he. *I'm elastic, I expand and*
contract, I won't pop
or crack, trust me . . . He runs seven businesses, all from
this one spare frugal
office. *How can you wear so many*
hats?, I ask.
How many citizens in your country?, his reply. *We have*
only three-hundred-forty-thousand in this wide flat land,

scattered to all outlying reaches. To serve the people,
a business must diversify.
Diversify.
One thing led to another. His
prized lemonade grew popular so fast,

no way could he dispense or deliver it quickly enough
to supply all the vast
network of orders without fashioning a state-of-the-art
bottle design. He built
six bottling plants bestrewn to all
far reaches
of the country. And he initiated a three-wheeler
motorized cart, which can hop over worst deep furrows

and crevasses of the remote outland, homestead of Amer-
indian tribes. His the sole
factory that
mass produces carts. So be it . . .
And for all his frenetic job details,
he has risen to the top rank in Jewish affairs. Heads
both the Israeli Consulate
and Jewish Utility Board, and finds a space to squeeze
me into his midday
whirlwind. *Why are all Rabbis
of Surinam
just half-trained?*, I ask. For over one hundred years
of Dutch rule, all *Ministers* of Jewish faith were church

ambassadors from Holland. And later, came emissaries
from America. Their training
was general.
One month, they held services
for Sephardic worshippers. The next,
Eshkanazi. Sermons almost identical. So the two leading
factions of Jewry—at odds
in Curacao and Aruba—grew closer and closer, in spirit
and customs. A fusion
of noted families came to flourish,

more and more.
Frequent intermarriage erased the barriers, or walls,
between the two camps. Today, since Independence, Rabbis

are recruited from the native tribe, no more volunteer
emigres from other lands. Chiam
Kopinsky,
just retired and pensioned at age
sixty, was half-schooled in American
Rabbinical college. The rest, he improvised on the run,
on the fly, between those two
clans—his sermons varied but slightly to suit most avid
sticklers in Sephardic
or Eshkanazi lore . . . *Jerusalem by*
the Riverside,
his ancestors dubbed the first hideaway Jewish temple
and settlement of the interior. They'd fled grim Portugal,

the scourge of the Inquisition hot in pursuit, branding
them heretics and demons.
Burning sands
of the desert they crossed—*BLACK*
FIRE—giving them harborage, welcome
sanctuary in the endlessly blinding sandstorm reaches.
If they wandered lost
in those near-trackless desert sweeps, they were saved
by vanishings, rescued
by their quiet disappearances, losing
their mad
pursuers to the fugitive winds. Chasing the chasers back,
ever back, to their oblivion of graspings. *WHITE FIRE*

LULLED IN GOD'S HAND PRINT

(Paramaribo, Surinam)

We stroll past the broad
expanse of Catholic wood cathedral—
largest church in the land, it counts more
active worshippers in its congregation than all
other sects. For years, the building has fallen deeper
into disrepair. *Now so rundown, that whole roof may collapse*
says Danny, if *the renovation doesn't proceed faster.*
Hunks of ceiling plaster and unpeeled paint curls
catch folks in the eye, or scalp, in mid-
morning service . . . Soon advancing
two city blocks to a lofty

mosque & synagogue
(side-by-side), we approach
the Jewish House of Worship. Doors
double padlocked and thick-chained. Alas, no
concierge shamas to give us brief
walkabout of the Temple's
interior. Danny,

who has paid his respects,
yearly, on Sephardic intro nights,
offers me a breeze-by spiel . . . We scamper
past two leash-tied black watch dogs (Dobermans,
snarling), who tug at their tethers, savaging the holy air
over their heads with menacing forepaw swipes, their squeals
half-hearted threats. *We come in peace*, chants Danny,
open hand extended—fearless, as a few scratches
behind the ears calms them to sad mewlings,
whimpers. The sandy grounds so freshly
raked in neat crisscrossing

rows, I must pick
my steps lightly. I could
be tiptoeing across thin ice sheets
over a near-frozen brook. I hate to defile
the sanctity of punctiliously exact
rake marks. Narrow lines
fall into rounded

edges and wide curves along
yard margins like huge hand prints,
as if the palm of God has gently brushed
across the sandy expanse, leaving its evanescent
markings (merest wind chops could reduce that pattern
to blank erasures), which hint of the Holy Spirit's indelible
underpinnings. *Who am I to despoil God's own fragile
hand pressings?* . . . Danny draws me after him. *Fear
not. The grounds won't bite. Never snapped
off anyone's toes yet* . . . I shudder.
Halt in place. Near the dead

18

center of sprawling
six-pointed-star of bricks
(DAVID STARR, the Dutch stone masons
and contractors have titled it), each star
arm perhaps double my height. By late
afternoon, I might cast
a shadow to match

its length. And still later,
my dimming shadow would much exceed
that star's longest arm expanse. All this
my swift musings, a whimsical fantasy unfolding
of itself as I stand—trapped—in the brick-by-brick
chain link clutch of Star of David's charmed mid point. Danny,
again, must coax me to cast off my *starry-eyed drift.*
Slowly I glide from the brick starfish embrace
A safety felt along those protective arms
In that magic circle, my breath comes
easy   My body gives up its

deadweight, its odd
foreign man's dull mass   My
plodding step grows light—so far from
home   My family strides near in the shimmer
Danny, my dark familiar, presses our
fellow feeling deeper   Ah, he
takes me by the wrist

So gentle his touch   He may
be leading a blind gypsy lost   A soul
asleep, just coming to, coming out   Now we
approach the temple front gates. With his free hand
he points to the wide archway above, and he implores me
to translate the Hebrew phrases engraved in the nearby overhang.
I sound out the few words, right to left, ever surprised
my accent rings true. My tongue's rust, or tarnish,
impedes—but I find my nuance, singing the Old
Testament syllables back from childhood
memory. Even so, my mumbled

miss-or-hit stabs
at English versions fall
wide of the mark, my ear's palpitant
grasp of the music near lost. A brain lapse.
Years of training buried in grey cell
idleness . . . Danny offers
solace. Here, too,

upkeep and repair lag, grind
to a standstill. The brick tool shed
and janitor's quarters, a squarish hut locked
behind the synagogue, is lacking most of one wall.
The storm-tossed thick tree limb, which cut a triangular
wedge in the wall's masonry, still hangs in the toothy zigzags
of the gap. Ten months since the collapse without repair
or patchup—a civic disgrace! Worse yet, horseplay
and pranks of vandals. He points to windows
in the temple front wall. Two cracked
by hurled stones. One upper

window—still intact—
fractured into a sad mosaic
of glass shards, held in the frame
by makeshift tape and glue. The lower left
window sporting a melon-sized hole.
That one rock heaved clear
through into chapel

landing on the velour covers
of chief Rabbi's throne. No worshippers
injured by the slung rocks, luckily—assaults
occurring after hours, those vandals never spotted
in the act. Who would do this? Who enemies of the Hebrews,
here? . . . Locked shut, the Jewish House of God is closed, today.
No access for friends or allies in the Faith. But we step
forward. *Let's have a look inside*, says Danny, who
boosts me upward to low window sill. Perched
on the ledge, I catch views of two low-
hanging chandeliers, each

encircled by three
tiers: three rows of candles,
fresh wicks—but rarely lit perhaps.
Electric lights brighten the hall and chapel
for most services, the candles saved
for high holidays. *When all
wax candles are lit*

at once, says Danny, *it's*
another world sprung alive. The rich
panels—varnished wood interiors—seem to glow
with their own eerie sheen. The candles kiss the wood
into a rosy glitter of the polished grain, and flashing wall
units flutter with their own light, he swears. Light that smiles
or grimaces, by turns, as song of the cantor wavers from joy
to despair. Music and light, one alters to fit the other
as if the singer's high notes and low notes be
mirrored in the candle glows. *And what*
a sight it is! At the peaks

of a high service,
those dozens of candle wicks
aflutter in sync with that cantor's
rapid glissandos . . . Once he beheld this vocal
light show, himself a guest at Yom
Kipper service. *Three rings of*
white roses ablaze . . .

THE POET ON THE POEM

"Chagall's Rabbi" and "Lulled in God's Hand Print"

Surinam (Dutch Guinea): I loved the music of the name "Parimaribo," so I crossed over the Guyana border to check out the office. A lean lanky boy of about 19 greeted me outside. "No official guide" Danny confessed, but he'd love to give me a "quick tour." I was stunned by the close juxtaposition of a small synagogue and mosque, two little huts side by side. Does this symbolize the good fellowship and harmony between historic enemies? I ask. "Not exactly," says Danny. In such a small country they must conserve space. The main Jewish House of worship can be found a few miles "inland." It's called "Jerusalem by the Riverside." Danny, not Jewish himself, is a careful observer. For a small donation of my own choosing (not a fee!), he'll give me a tour. We approach the Jewish Temple, careful not to disturb the line patterns in the sand. Every daybreak, an elderly caretaker freshly rakes the parallel lines in the sand. They appear to be markings inscribed by giant fork tines. But as I go stepping gingerly across them, I suddenly find myself at the center of a large six-pointed star encircled by the raked lines, parallel rows radiating out like star arms. I halt, frozen in place, as if in a timeless trance. I stare overhead. A wide hand descends, and soon, the beneficent open palm cradles me. I rise... Now Danny beckons me to leave the aura of the Davidstarr and come peep with him into the window of the Jewish Temple. The midday sun is bright, and I must squint to see the lovely menorah of unlit candles on the table inside. It is a pleasure to listen to Danny as he chants his vision of the spectacle of lights during the High Holidays each year. Yes, he is strictly an outsider, but a thrilled witness, even so.

Later, Danny escorts me to the modest home of the most exemplary Jewish man in this desert country. There are some 300,000 residents in this former Dutch Colony—no longer a satellite of Indonesia—but this national leader of all people of his faith is best known to the general public for his bottle factory, and the secret recipe of his brand of lemonade, a great favorite across hundreds of miles. Luckily for me, he is delighted to greet a Jewish American visitor. After our exchange of niceties, our talk quickly focuses on the one remarkable painting on his wall. "CHAGALL'S RABBI," he proudly declares. "It is the only such work." But no, I seem to recall that Chagall did several rabbi portraits. "Yes, but no," he says. This is the only one…in all of Surinam; no other Jews own any of those vintage Judaic Chagalls. He now reveals himself to be an aspiring biblical historian, well read in the Talmud. And he recites, from memory, an electrifying passage that charts many key milestones of the Jews' amazing survival across thousands of years of historic wanderings and wayfarings: the epochs of black fire and white fire, as reported in chapter and verse. And just last week the single African-Jamaican parishioner in our local congregation announces his scholarly discovery of the key passage in the Talmud depicting the various getaways and escapes from bondage across the desert by unnumbered generations of Jewish fugitives.

UNDYING IS AN ART:
SONG OF CAPTAIN HODGE

(St. Martin)

No work address or phone, but Tony's a *livewire*
of the small ingroup
    Spanish barrio of Phillipsburg.
       Check him out at the Spanish Bar, says my expat friend Sylvia.
On the beach. Near dead end
of Front Street. A message left there, at any hour,
    will find him quick as *Carrier Pigeon.* Keep checking back

      for him there at short
    intervals. He cannot stay away for long.
      That bar's a quiet artery
    and switchboad
      for all Spanish life
of the town. Tony Hodge, Tony Velasquez, by turns . . . When
      we meet there, two hours
      later, he's heard
about me from six different sources. How much
    he knows astonishes me.
No computer vitas
here, for locals or

    visitors. Strictly a word-of-mouth variant
of same. My former
  two visits, each six years apart,
    seem to have been engraved on the oral relay memory bank. Hey,
has he met me before? Can't

recall. But one David Lieberman was his Super
at *Eastern Qualfest Stapling Company* in Long. Island,

                    most generous and winning
            employer of his life. And David often
                promised to visit St. Martin
            for a reunion
                gig. So far, no show.
But I'm the *best next thing*, same family or not. *Not*, I demur,
            but embrace the welcome . . .
            Tony, fifty-
six and five times married, once in Saba,
            twice in St. Martin, once
in Long Island, N.Y.,
            and most recently

    in Santo Domingo. Eight years (his longest yet)
to Rosalina, mother
    of his once and only small son
            Austin, age five . . . But he must run off to round up distant
    cousins, nephews, aunts thrice
removed in Bonaire and Tobago for the pre-
            orchestrated—indeed choreographed—funeral and wake

            of his soon-to-die father
Captain Hodge, recently knighted by Queen
            Beatrix for twenty five years
    of distinguished
            service on the High Seas.
Will Johnson, Saba's famed author-senator, arrives tomorrow
                to deliver sweet tribute
            for last gasps

26

nonagenarian . . . *Who says he will die?*, I
　　ask. His long-time doctor,
declaring his *weak heart*
　　　　shant eke out one more

day . . . Hilltop vigil for languishing Patriarch.
In frontroom, four awed
　　generations of hangers-on. Kids
　　　　swarming about. Most relatives bidden from foreign ports—U.S.,
Canada, Holland, Curacao—
for expected funeral. Tony, the oldest
　　　　son, presides. Escorts me from room to room. Intros pile

　　　　　　up too fast. I can't keep
track of the relations, some infants uncles
　　　　or aunts to their grownup kin.
　　The overlapping
　　　　family layers, levels,
astonish the Grandame: our dying Captain's wife, Muriel. Even
　　　　　　she seems blurry-minded,
　　　　　　nearly stupefied
by the quantities of great nephews, nieces,
　　　　　　grandkids. It's like trying
　　to keep pace with all
　　　　those new characters

　　　　cropping up in Russian novels. We must start
back-flipping pages
　　to keep it straight. But here, niceties
　　　　forbid my asking for repeat familial titles and ranks . . . Next,
　　bedside vigil. I edge into
room of the elders. In far corner, the dying
　　　　man lies supine, face propped on pillows, eyes shut

under mosquito netting.
Is he awake, asleep, or comatose? The net
shrouds any feeblest moves,
and I'm too shy
to ask after his state.
Two women are seated on next bed's front edge, wife eighty-
one, and young sis' Rita,
seventy-nine.
I stand in the doorway, and greet them—one
by one—stepping forward
to shake hands, then
back, while Tony brings

me a chair. Muriel's older brother, Irving,
rises from his chair
between the beds—big smile despite
sore creaky back that unbends in five successive bobs and shakes.
At eighty-seven, he's next
family lodestar in line. He taps the shoulder
of his son Jody seated in room center, and bids us join

hands. Prideful, he croons:
Jody is our town's master Church Organist.
Since the Captain can't muster
strength to rise
from bed to waddle down
his zigzag path to Church today (first Sunday in seventy years
he's had to miss the Service),
Jody brings Church
to the Captain. He embraces his long folded
black case, lain out across
his lap. This implement—
in the shape of a sled

or short tobaggon to my view—is the portable
mini-organ which Jody
    often transports to devout churchgoer's
        sickbed. Not just last rites for the dying, but healing hymns
    for the convalescent. Some chords
and arpeggios from this source may have caught
        my ear as we approached the house a while back, then

            ceased as we neared front
    parlor, which I mistook for a radio's
        ultra-clear, keen reception.
        Surprisingly free
            of distortion or static
in this wooded hill-top setting . . . *May I please hear a sample,*
        I ask, *if it won't disturb*
        the slumbering
    Captain Hodge? On the second syllable of the sleep
        word, the translucent net half-
        concealing the stricken
            man ripples and oscillates

        and lifts off, rising from the bed as by some
queer ghostly power
    of its own, and we see the oldest
        forbear's cupped hand reach out, drawing the cord which dispels
    the diaphonous veil, his eyes
aglow and lips parted for speech, or is it song?
        Play it again for our honoured guest, ha says, *and I'll*

        sing the verses, as before.
    Thereupon, lanky and long-armed Jody pops
        open the long case and spreads
        the glistening

exposed ivories of quaint
keyboard from his lap across rose petals of flowered counterpane
at the foot of the Captain's
bed. The opening
chords of *Amazing Grace* sweep across the few
octaves of blacks and whites.
The tiny room thrums
and vibrates like an echo

chamber—a wide church hall or chapel, notes
swirling about our ears,
the sound magnetically amplified
as from an electric guitar. But plain to see, it's a wireless
box his fingers dance upon,
his touch light as a butterfly's wings, the room's
acoustics wild and rumbly in resonance. It shakes us

in our roosts . . . The Captain
unfolds erect in his bed, his lips parted
again, and he gives full-throated
voice to a hymn:
O 'til we meet 'til we
meet again
and if we don't soon meet
we'll meet at Jesus's feet
At that moment, seaman Hodge's
voice seems buoyed
by deep ocean swells. He's the surpassing life
force of the room (death's
undoing), we others
scraps of jetsam
flung hither and thither. . . .

THE POET ON THE POEM

"Undying is an Art: Song of Captain Hodge"

My wife and I were visiting with her older sister Annie during the last week's remission of her dying from cancer when this poem's title suddenly came to me. The poem was otherwise finished, and Annie's life spirit was clearly the strongest of us all. Truly powerful, an "undying" spirit. No quenching that light… I'd visited St. Martin twice before, sweeping back and forth between the Dutch side and the France side. To go from one to the other, we merely had to cross a street. I'd quickly struck up a friendship with Tony Hodge, who virtually lived in the busy Spanish bar of Phillipsburg (neither Dutch nor French). He grew fond enough of me to want me to meet his whole big family: it was just the right day for these many intros, since they were all celebrating his grampa's (their oldest living patriarch's) birthday. Captain Hodge – in bed, lurking under a veil -- was turning 90. It was an enchantment for me to pass through the many layers of family as we strolled from room to room, getting closer to the aging pinnacle of the family. Toward the finish of the chain it was most striking to meet Jody who carried and finally performed on a long boxed keyboard. An ambulatory organ. "If a man's too ill to crawl to church, we bring the church to him." He must not lose his concert, it would be his first unhymned Sunday in 70 plus years.

OPERA

Poised on a flat wide rock, scanning the blank sandy waste
$\qquad$ (dotted with cacti)
$\qquad$ beside the ruins of the Balashi Gold Mines,
Julio is moved to *Opera* his newest poem for me. His vocal

$\qquad$ timpani belted
$\qquad$ over the sun-baked terrain! Three

$\qquad$ driest years in memory scald
$\qquad$ all woody plants and tree barks to tinder.
He serenades, alike, near

$\qquad$ and distant cacti, two ribald iguanas
$\qquad$ slithering closer for ringside box-
$\qquad$ seats; birds, wild donkeys, sheep & goats.

$\qquad$ The whole procession of
$\qquad$ wildlife receive his lament as one with
their gambols and scamper . . .
$\qquad$ Julio, himself, a dark familiar. Voice
all grow tame amongst. A few
$\qquad$ minute pause. Silence. Now Julio begins

lifting and lowering his arms, his hands cupped
$\qquad$ upwards, as if leading band ensemble. Still
$\qquad$ wordless, I await promised translation
$\qquad$ from Papiemento to English. Thus, he explains
how much worse drought than usual
$\qquad$ (on average, seventeen inches per annum) shall

have prevailed in the last three years.

        Eight, three & six inches, one year's
rainfall pittance diffused, thinnest

        patterings spread out over this trio
of seasons. In the best of years, rainy
   spurts confined

to just three months—October, November, December. Current
        cycle, much the worst
  dry spell of the Century. Julio, raised on
a farm, still works his own small private menagerie, keeps

   grazing a few
bulls, sheep, goats. He weeps, in

  his verses' final strophes. Any
  poem is a message, says he. It must convey
our Spirit's vows and faith.

        No, he shall not pray for rain. Doesn't
curse the drought. Instead, he thanks
        the Good Lord for stifling the downpours,

since all trueborn Aruban
        farmers providently forsook their failed
crops in the Thirties and
        Forties, to work for the World's Premier
Oil Refinery. Or Balashi Gold
        Mines. No rain, no rain. That's our just

deserts, he translates. The poem accepts
        the driest Fate, resignation to parched days
without end. No apostasy by those

34

tenant sharecroppers. Julio's tears shed only

against the decades of paltry

husbandry. The Spanish early settlers—men of

some clairvoyance—had wisely quit,

abandoning the *Useless Lands*.

THE POET ON THE POEM

"Opera"

How Julio Maduro loved to recite his poems in Papiamento! He held forth across the wide plain of Aruba to his audience of listeners, all the wild animals of the isle. The farmers, of old, had all but given up during the last and worst drought. Rains in Aruba were always few and far between, at best, during the three wettest months toward year's end. But this year, there was practically no rain at all, so the last farmers left. Today, the whole island felt like Julio's personal and exclusive barnyard. When he recited his poems from the top of a little knoll, he imagined he was performing a grand opera for the scores of wandering quadrupeds. He even envisioned he'd hear their great round of applause when he paused at the finish of each strophe... There was a long history of farmhands who kept abandoning the island for lack of water. But the oil refineries and gold-miners thrived for many years, while sons of the old farmer class mourned the loss of that dying culture and demise of agriculture . . .

TRANSVESTITE

I must undo my robes of the air,
     untie my earth
  cloak
of foreignness, step out of my fear-being,
     ease into my sea
  skin
of a fish. I must enter my salt-self,
     drawing the smooth
  current
about me like heavenly drapes.
     A brainy stranger,
  I divest
crew cut and gold fillings, the silver
     ring on my wedding
finger
the water-tight wise ticker at my wrist
     proudly droning
  its one
secret to the wet world's deafness:
     Time's muffled
  bees' buzzing.
I must unremember my name, my birthplace,
     the number on my license
  plates,
my address, the brand of my children's
     toothpaste, the blessed
  earth-smell
of my wife's hair: to belong here
     I become a nameless
  dumb

free and easy man-thing. A presence
        infinitely deep
    blue-green,
full, rain-caressive, invites me,
        opens to one just
    opening
up, who, not now as a lame
        stranger, may
    enter.
I take in my hands all, all
        that I touch,
    and leave
no fingerprints. No signature.

PART II

THE LAST HARPOONER

1. GRANDDAD AND THE HUMPBACKS

Granddad Robert
Melville Simmons was first
mate on big U.S. whaling vessel
for three years . . . Later he shot a humpbacked
whale in Bequia's offshore waters (it was Spring,
nineteen-thirty-six), firing his rifle
from the bow
of a modest-sized fish sloop,
catching his two fellow deck crew
by surprise—
they doubting his resolve to put rude impulsive
first skirmish with local Leviathan
Humpback to wayward test.
Three shots fired,

third struck home—
missing the basking whale's
heart by a few meters, but deep wound
stunned him to a brief halt, which allowed
their near approach. Rifle froze, on reloading.
In his rush, Simmons crammed that barrel
too tight—the charge
blew up in his clutch, sea wind
luckily tossing powder spray & shrapnel
widely askew,
just clear of his face, while his chief mate flung
their one antique harpoon, nailing
twenty-five-foot beauty.
And it took that

whole afternoon
for the muscly trio to drag
& beach their amazing prey: she came
back twice from false death to yank the craft
half-submerged, but lacked power to sound down deep.
They held steady until she tired, then
slowly drew
her huge carcass ashore . . .
Earliest milestone in Bequia's whale-
kill saga! Rob
Simmons, forefather to the Isle's first generation
of whale-hunt buccanneers, soon renounced
guns for the harpoon and pristine
razor-sharp lance

he'd fashioned
and honed himself (new-minted
lance, over time, bore his name: patent
licensed by his family for thirty-plus years).
But apprentice whalers, *trigger-happy roustabouts,*
often resisted his wise tutelage
on the sly,
making the daybreak coastal
harbors their firing range. *A pitiable*
mess of whale
chasers . . . They toted any coarse handguns: pistol,
revolver, or old army rifles—castoff
shotguns: at best, grazing whale
fin or tail, and

scaring off
those few prize Humpback beauties
of the prime season . . . Granddad Rob coaxed
Nolly, age six, to join him and some thirty-odd
tagalong *watchers*, all early risers, for a hillcrest
hike. They wended & weaved through prickly
brush to a bald
clearing with stark lucid view
over fine pair of sailboats converging
from two sides
on a lone basking mound of liveflesh blackly ashimmer.
Pop Simmons—as his young cronies dubbed
him—drew three extra sets
of telescopic

glasses from deep
shoulder-slung pouch, passing them,
one by one, to his fellow beholders.
He bid the *blokes* to take turns. Circulate
that trio of *ocular aids* . . . But saved the keen-lensed
binoculars for himself and Nolly
propped on left
knee, as they sat on a flat
cliff rock. And he traded the glasses
with the child,
when the zings and crackles of gunfire rang out. Oh,
Granddad roared his disdain, his heckles
so shrill on the air, raw shooters
must hear it—

to no avail . . .
Shell-fire blossomed smoke plumes
unchecked. Pop took three deep puffs on fat
Cubana Cigar. Ejected bursts of sputum overhead
like sperm-whale's bubbly spout, his spit-line narrow
as a blowtorch. Then railed and grumbled.
Soul of chicken
farmers, that crew should be chasing
poultry, gamecocks—not Leviathans! He waxed
finical. Sloops
were angled false, came on too quick, rash scaraway
tactics . . . Whaling art laid down strict code.
No guns! Harpoon, or Pop's surgical
piercing lance.

2. ANGEL'S JAWBONE

Others assist. Only he throws the sleek harpoon.
Athneil, sole whale rider, whale
rodeo bronco buster.
He has telltale
scars to prove his solo prowess, solo
huntsman status. Scars
where ropes tore into his underlegs,
thighs, when they dragged
him many a time—stunned blind
or unconscious—

choking on backwash
of the flailing whale that blasted him skyward from a bow-legged
squat on its back. His eyes glaze over, then roll
like a punch-drunk boxer's, as he recounts a few most gruelling
whale-kill bouts, fierce

onslaughts leaving him dizzied or knocked-out, but
always springing back . . . For thirty-nine
years, Athneil has ever thrived
as Bequia's chief
whaler. Today, at seventy-two, he's legend.
The last harpooner.
O how he loves the whale-spume rodeo,
that one-on-one knee
clench hobble on whale neck (whale
skull?) in the sea

coliseum's match
of two towering gladiators. Athneil and your fifty-foot Humpback.
A fair contest. He bucked or shuddered off, countless
times, but always clinging to the harpoon-anchored rope, tugging
himself across slippery

slope of whale flank, again and again, as an expert
rock climber rappelling a cliff scarp,
then repositioning himself
behind the skull,
rotating his palms & clenched fists. A phren-
ologist searching
the contours of upper vertebrae to find
best entry point
for thrusts of his razor-sharp
lance . . . Our Athneil

the only veteran
whaler of Bequia who's scored a proven whale-kill with a single
harpoon plunge into the big cow's heart. None before,
in the one-hundred-ten years of whaling tradition, had taken out
a mature Humpback with one

flung harpoon. Straight through the heart. She sprang
upwards, bucked twice, swung over
on her back—and died in
less than a minute . . .
Forty-eight feet, twenty-five tons, her boasted
stats. Whale hunt award
of the decade . . . *And here's Angel's jawbone,*
he says. Suspended
over his gateway and mounted on
a silver plaque.

3. RELICS OF THE BONFIRE

Fifty footers. That's
your historic full-size limit for Humpbacks,
      local scuttlebutt drawls . . . But Athneil waxes pale
         over that one prize
    giant *who gat away*, three stout harpoons
& four lances speared deep
         into her blubbery hide. She grew more fierce
    with each wounding, sounded to unplumbed depths & yanked
  his famous battle-worthy boat (*Why Ask?*)
    down under—drowning
         two of his apprentice whalers. *Ah, she was*
    at least a sixty-five or seventy
         footer. So close

      to a score on mammoth
sea duchess! But Athneil—a strong swimmer—
    finally cut those three harpoon ropes with ankle-
      sheath knife, to save
Why Ask? and a few loyal crewmen still
clinging to her gunnels
    in most turbulent swells . . . Days later, live
  colossal Humpback flopped ashore on Guyana's southern
coast, whacking & pummeling beach pebbles
    with her wide tail—
      now impaled by upwards of a dozen harpoons
    & lances, snapping them all off
        in her travails

like puny splinters.
Lastly, drubbing herself to death on the level
strand . . . Word of a beached carcass quickly spread
to three Amerindian
tribes, miles apart, such marvel of shore-
dying grand Leviathan
luring scores of coast settlers from their huts
to feast upon some huge flesh mounds gratis for the taking.
Marooned Humpback whale, a first time gala
event for their calm
province: they began chopping & shaving off
choice parts with their machetes, setting
up small makeshift

bonfires, then roasting
all whale loin and whale belly sweet-oil globes
on the hot coals . . . Weeks after, rumor drifted North-
west to Athneil
in Bequia from the Guyana whale feast.
A miracle. Giant beached
Humpback which—a gift from the Amerindian.
Gods—beat itself to death on the shore, amazing fast self-
flagellation! So it appeared to three dazed
witnesses, one child
& two elder tribeswomen. Each local clan
took credit for the bounty, a reward
from deities

for communal good deeds,
their daily pure & clean living. Two day fête.
Followed by chanted prayers of thanks to the Gods,
tribal chiefs keeping
formidable large samples of whale bone
artifacts to parade
before their families, neighbors & rivals . . .
Athneil laments his robbed glory, lost fame of inflicting
death wounds himself. Both lies. Neither man nor Gods
could make true claim
of whale kill. In shore-trapped fury of its own
tail-and-fin poundings, Humpback Soul's ever
self-vanquished.

4. HOUSE OF BONE CHANDELIERS

(Bequia, The Grenadines)

I.

A number of cottages, spaced out along the roadway
         approach to Olliviere's
   ranch house, sport nondescript long
bone artifacts: one tied to a doorside lamppost, others

          strapped in tree forks
     or loosely dangled by chains
      from window sill, roof eaves, door lintel . . .
They have a slapdash
   temporary look—ornaments
      of a holiday or brief season.
      They adorn neighbor
shacks, whose owners or landlords—wishing
to partake of the star Harpoonist's fame—gathered
        prize castaway
        fragments of whale skeleton. Cracked
   or mildew-stained

bone parts, imperfect or missing a telltale joint end,
        but imposing for shape
      and size: they resemble long javelins,
broad shields perhaps, yet most summon whale presence.

      Whale afterlife aura . . .
   Patience, counsels winsome Scott,
   my driver. *Don't be fooled by false fronts,*

mere decorations
　　like Christmas tree tinsels.
　　　Wait for the full-fledged Palace of
　　　Honor . . . I'd mildly
gasped at a couple of bone-crisscrossed
upper entryways, as we neared that one authentic home
　　　site. His eyes
　　　aglow, our tall lean,
　　Stoic man

greets us at his gateway—main fence posts elegant, if
　　　　unflorid. He stands below
　　a highly polished arch, curved jawbone
of fifty-foot-long *Angel*, the only mature humpback ever

　　　　to have been killed
　　　instantly with a single flung
　　　harpoon. His hands wrapped around *Angel's*
outer margins, he
　　caresses the prized relic
　　　and invites my touch to the oddly
　　　prolonged icicle
　　shape at the center, which towers
　　over the widespread parabola base . . . Still amazingly
　　　unblemished
　　　and intact, like a tall white shaft—
　　ivory sculpture!

It's her nostril bone, he says. So lovely
        and crystalline, semi-
    transparent, but it feels firm as iron
to my finger's gentle taps. *Fear not, it's sturdy. Tough*

          as a bull elephant's
        tusk. Built to last . . . He trills
        the last word's T. Indeed, for a warrior
in his eighth decade,
    Athneil's a *tusky* robust
        specimen, taut and limber. Whatever
        his off-season
workouts, he stays in prime fettle
all year round. His own bone case, from anvil-shaped chest
        to oaken-brawny
        thighs, seems ageless. He balances
    on bare footsoles

as if always at the ready to spring into lance-hurl
          mode . . . House tour starts
    with a litany of wall-hung and wire-
suspended bulk skeleton parts. Athneil's *Whale Ivories.*

II.

A few rib bones
are laid out, randomly,
on his patio deck. A broad skull bone
dangled over the living room
entrance; displayed above, an embossed portrait
of his chief whaling vessel:
WHY ASK? A curved trapezoidal backbone
spread across that high wall over the mantel
piece. Five knobby thick segments
of neck vertebrae—
in graduated sizes—are stacked in formation
like a row of flower pots
along the wide mantel. A local sculptor,
perhaps, has burnished all edges
and slicked the hollows into neat grooves—giving
each a singular gleamy
finish. But the carefully linked row
suggests a wise whale head charging forward
as we stroll across the frontroom . . .
We exit through alcove
into a rear parlor and I duck—pure instinct—
to avoid being clouted
by the succession of whale models hung
from the ceiling like Calder
mobiles.
Imposing shapes.
Black silhouettes . . .
Right

Whale, sleek Killer Whale,
bulbous Sperm Whale puffing its bubbly
spout (eternally etched in that facsimile
of high fountaining spray), while
local Humpback Whale
completes the floating roster.
The last, if less
monumental, is clearly
more precisely detailed. The model,
homegrown, springs to life
with closely observed traits. The stench and aroma
of huntsman Athneil swirls
around the doll-like bust. It's the one
three-dimensional replica, the others all
poster art flatboard hangings.
Our host holds forth
upon the niceties of this species, no living
soul more intimate

with the Humpback than himself, so
often a sea jockey riding
on its back, primed for the kill. He takes the shape
of his whale-humping crouch,
enticing us into onsite peak moments:
arms spread akimbo, knees so outstretched,
legs in a crab-arched splits . . .
Man riding a camel,
an elephant, a stallion—each seat carries its
distinct holding pattern
and carriage. But whale-riding's unique,
Humpback Whale giving the squatter
an extra challenge. He acts out for us those famed
bucks, spills, flailings . . .

                              Ah, I
nearly missed the little whale, loosely hung—
    tethered from ropes at room's far end. *Blackfish*
        Whale, he says. This quarry, still
            beached most often
                with mere angler's hook-and-line at Old Sandy
                    Bay, St. Vincent. Caribs
                keep a low profile on this scarce
            breed—to avoid *Greenpeace*
        ravings, or game warden quotas. Blackfish, never
    plentiful but not *fished*
out, keep surfacing in season. Shrunk whale,
    like tarpon or swordfish, more a game sportsman's
        prize than true whaler conquest . . .
            Back hall gallery
                showcases a vivid painting of recent vintage.
                    It depicts the vaunted
                Nineteen Ninety Two near-catch
            of a recordsize Humpback,
        some sixty-odd feet, harpooned thrice by Athneil
    and his crew. But uncowed.
Unbroken. It sounded in deep waters, yanked
    WHY ASK? down with it, knocking four of six crew-
        men overboard. Athneil—still waving
            in command—planted squarely
                on submerged deck . . .

5. HUMPBACK, THROUGH A SPYGLASS

Cuthbert knew, at a glance, the whale was stricken—
like a ship that has lost its course,
it wobbled and swung
drifted in wild zags.
A great bulk of flotsam embraced by each swell,
and fighting them,
too, to regain its lost balance
and poise . . . Hopeless,
it must ride out its own body's
ponderous slow
flotations, a self-flagellant buoyancy that dragged
it toward shore. Surprised the blood
trail hadn't yet roused
the sharks, Berty
and his crew called *at ease*—their daily
quota of flounder
and mackerel jamming the hold,
that big surplus
flapping madly in the cargo
bins. They surely
had a record haul of hotel pricey platefish in tow—
no rush to blaze a sea route home
this twilight, for they owed
themselves a breather
and diversion for work cheerily well-done.
One and all,
they cast their lots to dally a bit
and tag along beside
starboard whale. It took no more
than ten minutes'
reckoning—by compass and rude measure of the wind

velocity—to divine that Ole
pained Blubber Flanks
was soon headed
for a forced landing at one of Guyana's
remotest beach
shorelines. Berty and Chuck placed bets
the strong tide'd carry
her ashore in just under an hour,
laggard time
they could easily spare for merriment, not to say
a chance to horn in on that manic
impending butchery
and plunder
of beached carcass. The Guyanese coastal
denizens little
guessing the colossal windfall
bobbing their shoreward
way on the tide currents . . . Tacking
cautiously
alongside Leviathan, Cuthbert gauged her size upwards
of sixty five feet, maybe thirty tons.
The largest humpback
ever spotted
(much less harpooned & captured) in these down-
isles Caribbean
reaches! . . . They kept maneuvering
to give the wounded
bull wide berth in the bloodied
waters. Sudden
lunge of the immense tail could swamp them.
Sail helmsman kept circling, edging
closer to the whale's
midmost flank,

which revealed two pulsing gashes just below
the hot-blood's heart.
When the surf-spray and spindrift
faded from view,
the mariner's small spyglass
that peeked over
the raw edges of those wounds, agape, and he knew
jagged style of gouge for handiwork
of his fellow Bequian
harpoonist
Athneal—who must be yowling heartbreak over
his record near
miss.

THE POET ON THE POEMS

Whale Poems:
"Granddad and the Humpbacks"

Whale hunt history. Big guns took out whales for many decades until the art of the harpoon and lance prevailed. The strict rules and rituals were as formalized as those for the bullfights in Madrid. The best hunters were admired and canonized as "buccaneers." At first daylight, the gallery of watchers were out on the rocks viewing with scopes the struggles of the lone harpoonist Athneil, who was giving lessons to his grandson Nolly – an avid learner of that near-lost trade and passion.

"Angel's Jawbone"

The jawbone of the biggest humpback ever to have been successfully harpooned was hung over Athneil's Gateway, a permanent tribute to his matchless prowess. Many other whale artifacts were nailed to the house-walls, both inside and out. To visit the house was to get the full museum tour, in which he touted record dates of both failed harpoon attempts and conquests. His 39 years of pursuing his heroic quest was a lone art, finally.

"Relics of the Bonfire"

I loved hearing about the great unmeasured size of the huge humpback that "gat away," trailing blood from its harpoon wounds for days and perhaps a hundred miles before flopping ashore on a beach of the forested hinterland of Guyana. Rumors have it that several Amerindian tribes fought over the spoils. Finally, several illustrious bonfires were held, attracting visitors armed with machetes and barrels or baskets along the sea coast. Such festivities had never before reached so many participants in the country's annals of whale hunts. Family legends abounded. Stories grew into myths or fables in the many cycles of retellings. No one knew which tales that were bandied about in families, or whole villages, were the true ones.

"Bone Chandeliers"

A whole scattered community of shacks lines the roadway approach to Athneil's bone-studded house. Many hovels, cottages, and sales-stands sport little carved chunks and joints of whale skeleton prior to the harpoonist's home. In his house, more a museum than family dwelling, charts and lists of milestones decorate the quarters, accompanied by a surprising overspill – sprawl and surplus -- of artifacts. Stories of the famed hunts are printed on circulars, handouts to the scores of visitors; often whole classes of school kids led by their teachers come to call.

"Humpback, through a Spyglass"

One particular narrative of an encounter between hunter and wounded whale stood out, above all others. It was a saga that traced and recounted close details of the chase – the hunter's eyes always remained close to the quarry with the spyglass. The heat of action was most personally intense in this piece, while side-by-side maneuvers of the hunter's boat tracked the chase. We felt the palpitations of close particulars throughout.

LARGESSE

Salt Cay's the tiniest isle
            in the chain, where most animals wander freely about—
      donkeys, goats, sheep, horses
   may turn up anyplace. Unbranded, none wears
            tags, but they know to whom they belong: where to drift
                  to be fed, that's proof
      of ownership . . . For hours before I spot even one elusive horse,
   Brian's four steeds keep bolting &
         weaving, skittishly,
            in and out of his ongoing spiel. So word-vivid they are,
      I fancy I'm seeing ghost
   horses in dust-puffs arisen by sudden winds
            behind the barn, or in dark shadows thrown by wave crests
near the pier; and I glimpse horse

            heads trailing wispy long manes in low-
hanging clouds. Now he chatters love quips to one named horse,
         ardently scolds another
for ignoring his commands—absent stallion
and mare, far out of earshot. They may have supersensory
            channels of interchange
with the frequent mutterings
      under his breath. A man in love
         with his equine beauties, if he talks to himself,

perhaps they overhear it
            in that *Beyond* . . . Brian's past birthright may offer
         some clues to this horsy-
   jabber trance. He hails from a long line
            of ranchers at the outskirts of Laramie, where he thrived
               on a fully engaged

horse-groomer Wyoming childhood, raising his two cowgirls.
The younger, his teenage daughter
        Cheyenne, today shares
            most chores cleaning the stables and farmyard. A prize-
    winning horsewoman, she gives
all riding lessons to visitors, and often leads
        early morning *First Light* trots and canters down the beaches
and shoreline trails. She's picked up

        quite a following in just three years
as trail-blazer, whole families from Canada and the States
        booking annual return trips
                to Salt Cay, mainly for followup horse-run
gatabouts with Cheyenne . . . Brian himself built the stables, working
                alone throughout a summer,
and still won't let assist-
    staff groom or tend the quartet
    of horses in any way. His guest-house provides

the only full-fledged stables
        in the Turks & Caicos chain, his four trotters alone
        proffered to visitors
for riding lessons or guide-monitored
        circlings of coastal paths and ever-changing trail routes.
            Nothing but the best
        for my noble steeds—Brian imports all horse feed: processed
rice from the Dominican Republic,
        organic enriched bran
            from Belize, having to pay both import tariffs & overlarge
        transshipment fees to relay
all foodstuffs through Providenciales, the Capital.
    Time to load feed stalls and summon the animals from hideaway,
he says, as we meander

back to the barnyard. With effortless grace
            he begins pouring into deep bins handfuls of bran from one bucket,
      then rice from the other,
                  all the while quietly chanting little love calls
to the distant roamers and drifters. Can he depend on their internal
                        clockworks to signal supper-
time, and magnetize them
      over to the food source? Still no show,
            which does not begin to test his patience, nor raise

his voice pitch or volume
            by fewest decibels. Confident he is, may even take
      heart from the challenge
of delays. Now his chants, at last, modulate
            to yodeling trills as he sweetens the call to mealtime,
                  naming them one by one—
            and how he loves their names, the feel of those monosyllables
snapped off his tongue. *Ah, come soon,*
      blessed Rip. Do hurry,
            it's time my dear Josh. Blue, come along, why don't you
      be first come, first served,
just this once, lovely Blue. I listen, listen hard,
            for possible hoof-taps' approach, but hear no sound risen
above Brian's heavy breath snorts

      while he works and hums a simple tune,
wordless now. And finally, he's hosing quick streams of water
      into a wide V-shaped trough,
            which starts him to murmuring gently, again,
and calling the names over his shoulder as he putters about, tinkering
                  idly with this fine-meshed

sieve, with that long rake,
  those word chants soon more intimate
    as if he's addressing his human kids, or grandkids.

So it's his Salt Cay family
      he lullabies and sweet-talks . . . I do recall that tonal
    register I'd picked up from him
on our winding sallies to the farthest ends
    of this triangular-shaped land, and back, in late morning.
      He was holding court,
    then, with the full local contingent of long-billed shore birds
which he named and tabulated
  for me on the fly—
    like so many cousins, uncles, aunts, come to greet us
  at a family barbecue, each
garnering their fair share of his fond endearments. Though ospreys,
kestrels and lizard hawks

  are—by all odds—his favorite breeds
among the grand year-round aviary that circles the skies
  over Salt Cay. Also, he's
    partial to the short-legged *pond-pickers*:
curlews and stilts, which, avoiding the seashore, constantly maintain
    their pecking at brine shrimp
and all tinier aquatic
  life forms in the retired salinas.
    He's been plotting ways to shift waters from pond to pond,

keeping brine feed ever fresh
    and salutary for all birds. As he named each species,

to one and all he hand-
wafted his barrelful of largesse, his wide paunch
        more an emblem of Brian's grandiosity than a mere stewpot
                of excess bellyfat. . . .
        At the steady gurgling of water in the trough, a first
tall-maned forehead comes peeping
        over the stone wall
                beside the stables before I hear any telltale hoofbeats
        of its lazy-loping advance,
its silvery neck glistening in the sun: he the foremost
        of Brian's handsome two stallions to make a showing. And yes,
Silver by name, the sole horse

        he hadn't addressed in his bleated calls
to feed-time, whether silver be normally the first to come round
    or if all four be so coddled
            and pampered, alike, they come at their own sweet
caprice. One by one, Rip and Blue—lithe sensuous mares—follow Silver's
            lead, sidling up to the trough
and food bins for long-necked
    dunkings, as Brian pats their flanks
        and massages each high forehead with a knuckle, in turn.

WHITE GOLD

I sample the topmost layers of gritty salt, scraping exposed
crystals with my fingernail—Brian pulling back my arm:
Wait, you must taste the pure White Ore. We avoid
that grimy outer shell. So saying, he pokes
a three-inch groove with his trowel
& scoops out Extra-
Virgin bright granules that I may
pop between my teeth. Even the best Kosher-
Deli salt, today, must pale beside this premiere
brand that finicky George Washington always procured
for his soldiers to best preserve their meats: White Gold

no bogus substitute
would be allowed in its place.
He gladly paid the island salter Czars
a pretty pence for their prime
undiluted stock,

though they kept hiking up the price. Twice, scam wholesalers
had tried to palm off inferior grades on the fledgling
President's scouts—swiftly both sellers of phony
Grand Turk salt were nabbed, fined & jailed.
And yes, the tart sting and pungent
aftertaste of bits
I sample, now, *are* keenly singular . . ..
The upper story of Morgan's saltworks rotted
and fallen into the ground floor, both upper levels
have collapsed into the basement storage shed at one end:
more a tomb or mausoleum to that aborted Turks & Caicos' Salt

Global Cartel
than any historic showplace.
The jagged, misshapen acres-wide hulk
of mineral crystals—stillborn
salt monolith

two-thirds underground—gapes from two tunnels. Brian & other
resident keepers of the flame help themselves, from time
to time, to modest scoopings of pure white stock—
at most, a barely detectable narrow dent
gouged from forty thousand bushels
that were abandoned
on the very day, hour, indeed minute
when the company went bust: all overseas
orders canceled, withdrawn at once. Then Bonaire
and Inagua, whose deep harbors afforded much freer access
to broad-hulled clipper ships, promptly stepped in and took up

all market slack,
dropping their export price
by half. Salt Cay's three-million-bushel-
per-annum *lifeblood* cut off
at a single stroke . . .

PART III

THE ST. KITTS MONKEY FEUDS

1.

Denholm, the Brimstone Hill Society's current
Vice President,
    who migrated from Mauritius to St. Kitts
        six years back,
    was ambushed by several clumped troops of Vervets—
wave after wave
    of *the varmints*—while jeeping uphill to work
        this morning,
    earlier than usual, catching the first light
at six: monkeys
    so thick on one stretch of road he couldn't see
        dirt passage
    ahead, no view beyond them, no view between

the dense clans,
    no way to count the hundreds—*the most I'd ever
        laid eyes on . . .*
    Denholm vowed never again to drive up here, alone,
at this hour,
    hardly knows what gave him such a fright: to date,
        no reports

    of monkey horde attacks on cars, or humans on foot,
but he rolled up
    his windows, fastened and battened down all canvas
        flaps of his jeep
    roof canopy, and cowered in his seat bucket, while
the chimp swarm
    slowly thinned out; a few juveniles sliding paws

over windshield,
    tongues lapping side mirror, teeth nipping aerial,
door handles.
    No shyness any more, they grow bolder and bolder—
        recalcitrant—
from twilight to dawn, then beat a wistful retreat

at full daybreak.
    Curious and balmy, playful they are, he surmises.
        No harm in it.
    But he shivers to think of their numbers, and oh,
how swiftly
    they multiply unchecked, no Natural Enemies to keep
        their overspill

in balance—as in their African homeland. "Our Vervets'
Happy Hour," says
    Denholm, "commences at dusk, just a few darkling shades
        past twilight.
    You may chance upon troops of thirty or forty, who
will freeze up
    at your approach, but they hold their ground: intrepid,
        not chary shy,
    as even months ago. They hang together. And if you
walk up to them,
    they seem to flaunt the new boldness in your teeth,
        won't even flinch
    at hand's touch, but I shant recommend you put them

to that test.
    It seems, they know they outnumber us by a wide
        margin already,
    and they may know that both Time and Numbers favor

their survival
    preponderance over ours—so I fancy: their tameness
        is never easy

    or just playful, but quietly embattled. A far cry
from domestic
    pets or zoo animals! That steely grim reaper's stare,
        eyes rivetted
    to some tree or view in the distance, always sweeps
past your face . . .
    O how they must know our Tribe's been gunning them
        down, failed try
    to decimate their population—they shall not quail,
nor forgive,
    believe it! And do not make household pets of any
        but the most wee
    newborns: once they come into their own full command,

autonomy
    in the wilds, it's too late to force a swing back
        to familial
    bent to humans—least to be trusted as playmates
for toddlers
    or infants, as all too often they are espoused,
        adopted. . . . ."

2

No word of the monkeys in guidebooks or tourist
brochures: natives seem to ignore them, why? I sense
a conspiracy of denials, or quiet dread,

lurking behind all monkey jokes tossed off, absently,
in the marketplace—town center or boondocks. . . .
Wild monkeys, so plentiful and easily trapped

with rudimentary snares, make the ideal subjects
for lab study. I devote a half day to tracking down
Vervet research camps, based in secluded forest

remote from the public eye—perhaps to elude
tourists & locals, alike. Three monkey task forces,
led by doctors and scientists, flourish in St. Kitts's

outback. The most recent encampment, of four years
duration, follows the tutelage of renowned
United States neuro-surgeon, who, seeking clues

to a cure for Parkinson's, concocts savage
experiments with caged Vervets (animal rights' folks,
without fail, stage their yearly mild protests):

drugs, electric probes & tissue carvings . . . Miles
inland and uphill, the Primatologists' camp
holds longest tenure—3 to 4 decades entrenched—

hellbent, til the 21st. Century, or longer,
to prove SPECIATION has turned its magic corner
in the St. Kitts wilds: *Evolution's Leapfrog*

to a total new species of monkey catapulted
before our generations' chosen eyes, sweet gift
for us all to witness (*his Eye* on Nobel Prize,

no doubt), the usual snail's pace of progress
from one Animal Gene Pool to the radical next one
down the line *sped up*—such is the lab team's

claim: accelerated, as it were, by wild swings
in climate, flora and fauna, soil composite,
et cetera. The Primatologists' findings,

all based on sizes and shapes of body parts, timings
of process or function, ill served they may be
to measure anything but the small mammals' slight

physiques! For such be the middling low regard
in which they're held, in secret, by that colleague
of a third neighbor camp: Montreal psychiatrist,

on extended leave from McGill Medical School's
senior faculty—here to explore the *Social
Dynamic* of monkey clans, free and on the loose

in their natural surround. A twenty year stakeout,
thus far, since Dr. Elkin first set out to delineate
a true and accurate Vervet *mental health model,*

for he would hope to draw many parallels, or psychic
links, between human and monkey social relations,
whereby to cast fresh light on symptoms of incurable

Depression and Paranoia . . . Doc Elkin's arrival,
delayed an hour by overlong meanderings in the bush,
I feel the aura of his approach before I hear

wispy voices in the distance, a garrulous prattle
not unlike monkey gibber: phantom elder trunk
freckled ash-white sweeps dancelike past fronds

& tall stalks of foliage, long arms looping high
overhead, shoulder moves in sync with his voice pitch,
upper body twists enhancing the rigor of speech.

Vocal lessons, I hear: snatches of pedagogy
extemporized on the run, to guest or young apprentice,
alike . . . Well fooled, was I, by his native staff

& domestics: *he not on island this week him travel
for days, months*—this spiel a protective sheath
to guard him from snoops, newshounds, jealous rivals

myself . . . But no specter or mistful ghost: this advance
of a robust, high-stepping broad figure bare-chested
longwhitebearded silverhaired hanks ringleted

over shoulder outblazed by tousled-fur whitetipped
shiny curls, thickish pelt of chest hair (*new species
of monkey, indeed*) . . . I catch him visibly wince—

by a keen face muscle effort control it, his strong
revulsion contained—to behold me, perched on porch rail,
pencil and notepad at the ready, he much practised

in dispatching the likes of those who would violate
the quiet nobility of his task. But I see his repugnance
pale and sink upon clasping my hand-proffered plea.

3

Only five
minutes, perhaps ten,
    can he spare to hold forth—a minilecture
    on his two decades, thus far,
    of monkey research. Mid Seventeenth Century, our

        Vervet story commences.
      French military bosses, who maintained
        the colonial outposts
    in French West
        Africa, sent all lower class
            infantrymen and cadets to Gambia
      and Senegal ("pits of the Continent"), where worst
        diseases of that Age were running wild.

    In soldier families, monkey pets grew
    so trendy, no wife would stroll to local park or market
without her pet Vervet
    perched on forearm or shoulder, puffball baby
    curled in straw hat's wide brim, perhaps, as in classic oils
and charcoal sketches of the period; or coupled
with human infant

in doll buggy,
two exemplary sets
    of ears bobbing over the side bar: the pink,
    the white-furred, black flat nose
    peeping out . . . When France lost sea wars to the Brits,

      Senegal and Gambia were
      the first poker chips to be traded at Treaty

Auction; the British Royal Navy
wives and kids,
    allured by the classy French styles,
        inherited those prize house pets, monkeys—
    first imported to Barbados & St. Kitts, unnoticed,
        perhaps, since one or two pets per family,

    at most, migrated, and no census records
    were kept, nor quarantine limits set. Monkeys, like pet cats
or parakeets, were ignored
    by perfunctory customs and immigration
    officials of their day. . . . So began the vast monkey clans
of Barbados, St. Kitts and Nevis, what with slightly more
than a thousand chimps

imported
to start with. Barbados
    drew the line first, forbade any new influx
    of monkeys, twenty years hence:
    a total ban, backed by threats of huge fines and jail

      sentences, since Vervets
    had multiplied so fast in Mount Gay province
      where a first soldier encampment
and military
    colony let a few monkey pets
      escape: then, mating freely in the wilds,
    they proliferated like crazy bacteria. In no time,
      the bite they took out of agriculture

    hit like a plague, or early hurricane
    ravishing freshly bloomed fruit & veggies. By Seventeen
Hundred, it was too late

to control the population explosion.
　　Vervets ingested at least one fourth of their body weight
per day, menaced all crops: watchdog stakeouts were left
overnight to patrol farms

against hordes
of the marauder monkeys—
　　snarly curs tied to long ropes, which kept them
　　in range of ripening fruit.
　　But monkeys outwitted the wardens, stripped all plants

　　　　nearing harvest, just outside
　　the orbit of doggie twines, while staying free
　　　　and clear of the growlers'
　　nips, immune
　　　　to barks and howls. And at last,
　　　　　　the monkey troops planned raids, cunningly
　　　　(if we had printouts or blueprints of their sorties,
　　　　　　they'd serve us well at pro-football lineups,

　　or small scale military skirmishes);
　　while one squad of Vervets taunted a patrol mutt, held him
at bay by swiping at his ears
　　or muzzle with outstretched paws, another flank
　　cut behind his tail to zip through a row of Christophene
globes or grapefruits—so quickly were all shrubs
stripped bare, even those nearest

the stake-chained
sentinel . . . Thus, by turn
   of the Century, all three governments banned
   the monkeys from their shores—
too late, no way to banish wild platoons of the bush.

     Few more than one thousand pets
    had slipped into all three isles, while today
      we estimate their number
much in excess
    of fifty thousand in St. Kitts,
       alone, more than the combined human
     census of Nevis *and* St. Kitts, as of Nineteen Ninety.
     If the monkeys multiply by quantum leaps,

   so, today, do the legions of bounty
   hunters, hired by police chiefs of St. Kitts and Barbados.
This thriving new career
   sector provides fresh employment, steady
   and lucrative, for perhaps a third of the idle workforce
who get paid twice—once by the State for each head
of slain prey, yet again

by our food
processing plants, which skin
   and butcher the carrion for its pricy meat,
   though the hides be worthless.
Of late, local Animal Rights activists are "sorely vexed,"

     their diatribes of outrage
    against the monkey massacres fast heating up
      in Underground Press, protest rags
    forbidden sale

to foreign visitors or tourists.
    The Prime Minister, hoping to offset
groundswell of public spleen, floods the town civic
    centers, markets and rural outback

  with thousands of colorful broadsheets
  and fliers proclaiming a pale justice: since Vervet monkeys
have *pillaged* and *despoiled*
    most farmers' prime fruit and veggies crops,
    the valuable food source must be filled by fair quotas
of monkey sirloin, monkey flank steak, not to downplay
fine monkey stews & soups

which become,
today, a gourmet delicacy
    in best chefs' recipes—fit to rival green
    turtle soups, famed worldwide.
The town councils, in turn, sponsor award competitions,

      prizes for new hit songs,
    top stories and poems, rhymed and unrhymed,
      free verse, holstering the virtues
of monkey foods,
      monkey eaters: vitamins, nutrients,
        plus new antibodies building immunity
    to a vast catalog of ills and diseases—all credited
      to our beneficent monkey-rich diets.

  A whole mythology springs up at grassroots
  carnivals—new folklores, in form of songs, riddles, proverbs
and children's bedtime tales
    extolling the monkey food panacea. A series
    of free pamphlets and chapbooks are printed, touting health

gains from the new Wonder Drugs, antitoxins,
refined in local chem labs

from monkey
glandular secretions, monkey
    blood serums; while monkey-derived powders
    and tablets are offered for sale,
    dirt cheap, in local pharmacies, widely held to curb

        many common or exotic ills,
      alike: doubly ironic, since both Senegalese
        and Gambian Green Vervet Monkeys
    are supposed—
        by many medical research teams—
            to be original carriers of the Aids
        Virus! Hushed rumors, these, can hardly dampen bold
           War Cries bellowed at our public rallies

    by paid factotums who kowtow to the Chief—
    threefold slogans, the popular catchwords: *Longevity. Wisdom.*
Sex Potency, all promised
    to those who consume sufficient minimum
    daily dosage of monkey protein, or monkey serum elixirs,
which can be imbibed, today, at small cost
in many popular sodas,

canned *Purée*
of Vervet Gland extracts,
    and food byproducts. Superior athletes, some
    quoted in ads on radio or TV,
    others quoted on labels of bottled monkey oil supplement,

make repeated claims—new record
wins in races and soccer matches are best enhanced
by monkey foods, which surpass, even,
the illegal
steroids, but without health risks
of the latter. All current Star Testimonies
agree! Monkey's choice Manna for long distance runners,
swimmers, bikers & muscly body builders. . . .

4

Kittitians feed on them. Vervets, ever, the most populous
monkeys in disease-
ridden countries of the African Continent, hardy
survivors for the many past Millenniums,
these, *our durable forbears,* be touted by the Islanders
as Health Food—
but to justify mass killings and butcheries,
the forests all one
sprawled

slaughterhouse. . . . Hunters disembowel & skin fresh-caught
bounty on the spot,
hoping to command higher returns by selling directly
to the general public—folks met randomly
at roadside, or in the bush. But mad outcries, vile clashes,
on increase
of late, keep erupting between monkey headsmen
and those families most
endeared

to their monkey pets, six or seven to a household perhaps,
monkeys, cats & dogs
all at play with human kids, indeed the whole nursery
behaving like offspring of one elder dog
or cat—the children loving them like human siblings!
Schizoid traumas
now develop, to one degree or another, in most
family homesteads,
monkeys

still the most popular domestic pets. How difficult it becomes
        for rugged grownups,
    much less children, to reconcile their monkey brethren
      with widespread monkey carnage and massacre,
   even on principle; but when the voracious bounty hunters
      take sniper
    pet shots at family Vervets cavorting with infants
      in houseyards or school
        playgrounds,

the parents—irate vigilantes—vow to avenge the wild shootists'
      transgressions. . . . *Worst case*
    hits cited in the news. Deputized huntsmen, called up
     before government magistrate, must answer
   to grim charges: gundown of baby monkey astroll hand-in-hand
      with child owner;
     tree perch hunter shoots monkey in arm's-embrace
      of child, his stray shots
        (bullets

misfired, so he pleads) striking dog and pet bunny; last case
     the most scandalous
   on the Civil Court Judge's docket: child herself winged
     twice, one cartridge lodged in left shoulder,
  the other, mere flesh wound, nicked her thigh . . . No child kills,
     child disablings,
    as yet, but grave incidents of juvenile hits
      by *stray cross fire*
        (though most

wounds go unreported for fear of repercussions, hunter reprisals
                against whole families)
        show marked increase, week by week, as government pressure
            to decimate the wild monkey clans, mounts.
        Bounty hunters get away with all-but-murder, so much license
                to kill prey,
            no limits, few penalties they be held subject to.
                The State Coffers
                    pay out

highest wage to hunters who gun down a hundredfold per week;
                but for all the thousands
        killed, thousands eaten, thousands butchered & meat canned
            in new local canning plants, or bottled monkey
        loins pickled with herbs & spices, fermented oil-based recipes
                run amuck,
            the Vervet multitudes are barely diminished. Today,
                green monkey throngs,
                    more fecund

than ever, seem to burgeon everyplace in the bush, much nearer
                the village environs,
        and rash monkey shootings threaten to jinx the tourism
            industry. Areas near town centers frequented
        by tourists, high-risk zones, are declared strictly off limits
                to roving hunters:
            if they be witnessed picking off monkeys by upper-
                echelon dignataries
                    from France,

Britain, Canada, or the United States, they must face penalties
                much severer than those
        prompted by sniper fire killings of family pets. Vacation-
                giddy tourists' public vented outrage, even,
        may cost sharpshooter huntsmen their lawful bounty license . . .
                In Barbados,
                St. Kitts & Nevis, perhaps by joint edict of councils
                in all three nations,
                        restricted

areas are zoned and beflagged out-of-bounds to Vervet hunters,
                on pain of large fines
        and prolonged license revokings. Yet most monkey-populous
                sectors, such as the original Mount Gay region
        of first wild monkey colonies in Barbados, are ariot with rival
                bounty hunter
                factions, each positing their exclusive territorial
                boundaries: who defy
                        other gangs

to cross strict borders & risk machete-hacked limbs, like Big City
                Western drug cartels
        and gangland mobsters slicing up the pie of prime city buyers,
                guarding each wedge of pie crust with their lives
        on the line . . .. But all hunter carnage has barely put a dent
                in three isle
                monkey populations, still far surpassing the human
                numbers, hands down, due
                        to absence

of Natural Foes, replete in the African outback, where green Vervet
         hordes are held in check
    by some five species of spotted cats, in all sizes, who
         can outrun them on the ground, out-trapeze them
    in the treetops—acrobatics the realm of quick survival jousts,
         not riflery
    and gun marksmanship. Ourselves the only slayers here,
         we men poorish stand-ins
              for leopard,

tiger, margay, cougar and jackal . . . Meanwhile, city folks applaud
         those armies of bounty
    hunters taking up the slack of unemployment, which provides
         a revenue boost for social services, plus money
    gains for hurts of the economy. But the bush-war crisis worsens
         in country home-
         steads, where three or more generations of Vervets
              have flourished as full-fledged
                   child partners.

5

Dr. Elkin builds his research quarter to open into the wilds—
   his vantage a doorway or window
  to the monkey's natural habitat:
  no cages, no zoos,
 no confining the specimen of study
to a quarantined lab.
In his own glide of person, blent into backdrop, he's hiddenly
   visible—as hunters be shrouded
  from bird view on lake face,
  ensconced in duck
 blind: who has devised a unique walk,
half hip rotation,
half back-and-shoulder whirl, more akin to monkey's locomotion
   than any human's I've yet beheld;
  while his lungs, drawing breath
  a softer way, keep
 the monkey clans tame and fearless
of his free-swishing
advance. Himself a mobile Eye, passive uninterfering witness,
   he takes in the shuffle, reshuffle,
  of all norms in the Vervets'
  social milieu.
 Most wayfaring monkeys, at large, prowl
freely in the bush
when no scavenging bounty hunter looms near. They meander
   in flocks. Troop size ranges
  from eight to forty—perhaps
  twenty, on average.
 The larger units, more sedate, installed
in partial homestead,
cohere around an eldest female—the Head Matriarch revered

as a command ambience, or Guru.
Nearing peak size, a dominant
young male lures
frisky handful away, forming splinter herd
of eight to twelve,
who, in turn, pick up solitaries, gathering forces to become
a full-fledged troop of twenty.
But in times of clan turmoil,
they reconnoiter—
timid and sheepish—back to their home base,
to beg sage counsel
in form of calming nods, gasps, sighs by the reigning Queen.
And she does quell the hysteria,
restoring balance with her soft
tempos, deep reserves
(*such power aquiver, you'd suppose she wore*
crown, waved a wand:
literal scepter might be the stripped shiny branch she flicks—
you must see this queer masquerade
to believe it), while she squats
in tree-fork throne. . . .
Soon the renegade herd splits anew, perhaps
adding new members
to its ranks. A normal midsize troop—which fast proliferates
into moderately stable unit
some six weeks to two months
after first rebels
break from the pack—comprises near equal
numbers of males
and females; but no fewer than two thirds shall be juveniles,
which gives a reliable quotient
of how swiftly Vervets breed,
no keeping down

their sex play or frenetic propogation . . .
"Wait long enough,
stay quiet," says Elkin. "You may catch them in mating frenzy.
            It breaks out like your soccer
        match at the half-time bell.
        So sudden it is,
    no early warning signals we can pick up
(my personal radar,
at least, not sensitive enough): wideopen orgy! Mostly hetero.
            Youngest mate with oldest. All
        combos Gung Ho. Hots keynote—
        frequent switcheroos,
    rotation of partners so swift & constant
we cannot track
the turnabouts: sex relay teams! Juggling acts, whereby sleight
            of hand befuddles your eyes'
        tardiness. Vervets perennial
        random maters:
    in humans, we'd call it promiscuity carried
to the Nth. Power.
Indeed, as we watch the verve & gusto of mating circus heat up,
            mate switches seem to explode,
        incrementally, on the upside:
        Quantum Leap
    sex bouts, I'd term it. Gibbons, you may know,
the only Primates
proved, to this day, to be truly monogamous: but Vervet monkeys,
            though not known pair bonders,
        form tightly-knit ties, always,
        within their troops.
    Once the Clan unit is fixed, they remain
loyal to the clique
for long durations. Though splinter groups are led by dominant

youngish males, the larger droves
drift back to matriarchy,
once a revered
elder female emerges—groomed to be Empress.
Whenever herd size
grows to twenty-five or thirty, the queen hunt process unfolds.
Three or more candidate rivals
may primp & dazzle, but Vervet
Grande Dame
comes into her own, and her firm hegemony's
never in doubt.
She reigns for *Life Term*. Wrongly, we presume our family ties,
social mores, are more civilized
than norms of the *lower* Primates.
Given the lie,
in St. Kitts. Take nursing Vervet's instinct
toward mutants,
mental retards or deformed offspring—she adamantly refuses
to feed or care for that deviate
babe. Her troop says a flat Nay
to aberrants,
won't tolerate dull-minded newborns—starved
and left to die;
monkeys one-up on humans, since they improve genetics of Race
by weeding out feebler strains.
If borderline case be in doubt,
the troop consults
our Grande Dame: she, tie-breaker to the last,
ends the deadlock."

6.

Dawn after dawn, Elkin scrutinizes
　　the Vervets'
　　　　communal life in the wilds. He discerns,
　　　　　in time, the clear-cut checks
　　　　　& balances at work in the troop: slowly, he feels
　　his way toward their full range of mood swings—

　　　　he can target
　　　　　early signals of an upcoming storm turbulence,
or pick up happy gush
　　of affect, those electric surge highs
　　　　when good feeling spreads to all corners at once
　　like sun breaking through cloud.
He comes to sense the next shift, moments before,
　　　　and finds he can predict all near-term social weather

changes, much as uppers or downers
　　in those human
　　　　families he monitors in group therapy
　　　　　sessions back home in Montreal.
　　　　Rather, his powers to intuit the monkeys' psychic
　　climate improves, with the passing months,

　　　　since the remove
　　　　of a few species jumps, the smidgins of genetic
distance between Vervet
　　clans and himself, gives him a clarity
　　　　and balance wanting in his intimate closeups
　　with humans he so often failed
to help, much less cure, in family counseling.
　　　The Vervets, in most fleshly and metabolic leanings,

mirror us: our exact matchups, even,
for high blood
pressure and alcoholism; in both cases,
their population averages
a mere 5%—like ourselves—the ratio per hundred
who are most vulnerable to addiction

or illness: hence,
the great value of Elkin's research to depict
a near accurate monkey
health model. His work in the St. Kitts'
bush commenced on pretext of drawing parallels
to humans; but, of late,
his research leanings have tugged him away
from the human psyche to pure inquiry of Vervets'

social habits. Yes, their society's
mind order
is subtle and complex, which eludes,
utterly, his colleagues
in the neighbor site, *hung-up on speciation theory,*
who measure skull sizes, tweak muscles, etc.,

ad nauseum . . .
Thus, Elkin would hope to dispel much falsity
in monkey folklore, lies
borne of local politics to support
the war on Vervets, those limitless slaughters;
still worse, the lies fostered
by *fool species-change claptrap.* For five years,
he's been putting to his own private test the suspect

case for NEW SPECIES OF VERVET EVOLVED
    IN ST. KITTS,
            soon to be documented in publications
                penned by *local hooligan*
            primatologists . . . Months back, their camp imported
    unspecified quantities of rare African

             monkeys, strains
              believed to be direct ancestors to our Vervets,
whereby to shore up their weak
        findings. They set about to collect
           raw data of process and function, as measured
      by clumsy body gauges, tests
geared, strictly, to one monkey at a time, one
           by one by one, battered by machines, electric shocks,

      drug injections: the poor lab animals
          pushed to extremes
              of hunger & thirst; their muscles, tendons
                stretched to all limits,
             and beyond, for speed and endurance. But never, alas,
    are two or more creatures viewed in a free

             non-lab setting,
           or natural habitat. Now Elkin hires out a dozen-odd
Vervets from diverse imported
        strains, tagged for his private study,
          while the bulk of his fellow researchers travel
      abroad, one noted scientist
leasing subjects from others *in absentia*—who
         treat the small animal stockpile like a lending library.

First, he commingles six African chimps,
    a mixed blend
        of several imported strains, in enclosed
            outdoor space: a wiremesh cage
            encircling trees and shrubs in the wild, to simulate
a natural locale, as in best modern zoos.

        And he repeats
        this trial and error Vervet population mix-up
with several different troops
    of both imported and native monkeys,
        always in equal numbers—a twinning of foreign
    and local teams, so to speak;
the results are always the same, like magic.
    Local Vervets, strongly dominant, come out the winners

in group free-for-all, get the largest
    share of food
        & drink; champions, too, in rare slugfest
            mostly settled on squeals
        and bravado of arm wavings, body slaps performed
on themselves, as though to mimic human

        wrestlers' chest-
    poundings to scare off all wouldbe opponents.
Kittitian Vervets, then,
    seem to vanquish their Senegalese
        adversaries in all contests of aggression.
    Next, if the balanced mix
is left *in situ* for still longer durations,
    a curious pattern of mating habits unfolds, slowly,

but decisively. Two or three discrete
    African strains,
        who resist all impulse to interbreed,
           soon begin to copulate
        with Kittitian monkeys: transcontinental mating
    flourishes unchecked. Again and again,

        most Overseas
        monkeys prefer the Island cousins as mates,
repulse their home buddies . . .
    Ever a shrewd observer of monkey
        semiotics, Elkin studies the pattern of cues,
    grunts, whinnies, snickers,
as well as hip swings, shoulder lifts, arm twists—
    all forms of body language he's learned to decode

from years of close scrutiny in the bush,
    Elkin's skills
        akin to deciphering a foreign spy system's
           code, flag-wave semaphors,
        or suchlike. All local chimps and imports, he notes,
    fail in joint efforts to communicate

        with each other;
        most cues and signals fly past, sadly go over
the alien sex partners'
    heads. The pain and frustration of lost
        signals, misfires, is obvious in puzzled faces,
    head shakes of quizzical
wonder—yet the mating allure grows strong, ever
    stronger: the crux of Elkin's case against speciation!

7

Of late, Elkin's appalled by a shift to great numbers
of underpaid
        mercenaries, joining the St. Kitts monkey war posse
                and bandwagon
        (*hundreds of unlawful immigrants, no doubt, imported*
for dirt low
        Black Market wage by the government)—to save revenue.
                If divulged
        by the Press, or leaked out to the Populace, the shock
may undermine
        the Town Council's chief rationale for the dramatic
                speedup in pace
        of monkey slaughters: well-paid job detail for hundreds

of unemployed
        native workforce veterans, not to say poor retirees
                living from hand
        to mouth, after a lifetime of able-bodied service.
Perhaps dozens
        of these, it seems, shall now be bypassed, to favor
                those dirt-wage

        hirelings, escaped criminal types, homeless wayfarers
from isle to isle,
        no job too tawdry, no pay scale too scant . . . Inured rage
                of local farmers,
        exacerbated by the marauding monkey hordes' fierce
devastation
        of prime fruit farms grown worse this year, tends to fuel
                the Ruling Party's

political mandate and clout in escalation of the War
on Vervets,
    more tax revenues earmarked for the battle, looser
        hiring policies
    indulged. . . . Granted, the monkeys—epidemic or menace—

must be stopped
    from devouring St. Kitts' farm crops! All the same,
        I ask, pleading,
    if the Doctor and his scientist cronies encamped
in far outlands
    can persuade the Prime Minister to try to find a way
        to save the Vervets

    from brutal massacre. Well yes, he and his close peers
have kept lobbying
    to persuade the VIPs to pay bounty hunters, instead,
        to take monkeys
    alive—catch them in nets and snares, employing modern
tactics developed
    by World Zoo Commissions: baits in pits, or luring them
        with fragrance,
    scents they can't resist, doping them for easy capture,
then stockpiling
    thousands of monkeys in kennels, wide tall cages, stored
        for worldwide
    sale to zoos and research laboratories. Elkin claims,

there's enormous
    demand abroad for Kittitian Vervets, in particular;
        their Overseas
    purchase, if promoted as revenue-strong local industry,
would rejuvenate
    the Island's shaky economy far better than selling
        dead monkey meat

    for food . . . But his proposals, struck down by the lower
courts on vague
    technicalities, never reach balloting for free vote
        referendums.
    The Cartel smuggling mercenaries into St. Kitts, much
the stronger lobby,
    cannot be stopped. And too many vengeful citizens, needing
        a Blood Sport
    Cathartic, crave the ongoing hunt and kill to punish
the perennial crop
    destroyers. Elkin continues to tout the great demand
        for live Vervets
    in foreign markets—for guaranteed lucrative returns:

a Big Business
    could be nurtured, which might quickly rival Batik works,
        historic books,
    sugar and shrimp, as St. Kitts' leading export. But the air
is thick with Feud
    Musk, the soent of carnage, revenge, a tough momentum
        to turn around.

8

This year, alone,
    the vanguard of government-paid full time
bounty hunters has tripled—
    only two or three prime zones of tourist capers
        are off limits to the Death Squads. Huntsmen now work
        in small battalions
            back in the bush, since monkeys are ambushed,
often, in droves of forty, and hunters want to make a clean sweep
    of lucky run-ins,

    who seal off the pack
    by encircling Vervets' hideaway or bivouac,
thereby to lose no stragglers . . .
    A common horror—I'm told by youth Animal Rights'
        chaps—is to spot a dozen Hit Men bursting from forest
        thickets at daybreak
            lugging on backs, shoulders, heavy baskets
or net bags, so brimful of monkey carrion, the overspill surplus
    of stuffed-doll shapes

    leaves a grisly trail
    of corpses in its hurried wake. If, absently,
you ignor their beeline route
    from mid-forest outward to valley clearing,
        you could mistake the pack for fishermen bowed down
        by a record haul:
            bushelfuls of amberjack or yellowtail, say,
whole schools of gamefish netted & yanked from the sea in
awesome
        swift ten minute plunder

of the pre-dawn Bays,
    as often happens at peak fishing season.
But these crews ne'er display
    the eye sparkle and bronze-cheeked allure, necks
        upreared like prancing stallions of the happy fisher
            fleet: proud heroes
                flaunting their great catch to dawn choir
of cheerers, the first arrival of housewives on foot, by donkey,
        wagon or motorcar,

    to claim fresh flappers—
    most of the batch whipping about in barrels
or nets, as if fighting off
    a tad of unexpected turbulence and rough currents
        at sea, then to burrow back from bay whirlpools to open
            waterway. But no!
                This quarry of bulk carcass is *stock still,*
the haulers puffing, faces averted from passersby, eyes downcast,
            no social pride aglow

    in this workmanship,
    no matter how deft or expert has been the kill . . .
After two decades encamped here,
    Doc Elkin knows every local face. So hunter lads
        hide their visage from his glares, whenever he crosses
            their paths, by chance,
                on his morning, stroll: blood of massacre
yet steamy in the air, bloodstains mixed in sweat of their brows,
        adrip from leaky baskets.

THE POET ON THE POEM

"The St. Kitts Monkey Feuds"

Perhaps my strongest poem, ever, sprang from an unlikely twist of fate. My wife, who had been for many years unwaveringly supportive to my wild range of writing projects, took a vehement stand against my plan to write about the monkeys in St. Kitts. We'd heard that a notable Canadian scientist had set up a camp on the island to study the rapidly proliferating society of vervets. We spoke to a couple of his associates, who clearly were intent on warding off "tourists" eager to harass their mentor with questions. They claimed he just left St. Kitts and was not expected to return for a month or so. But I distrusted their tone, and kept returning, at intervals, to the edge of the woods they guarded. My wife, whose father was a brilliant radiologist, grew angry. It was a mystery to me at first. She wanted me to give up this quest, fearing I would distract the scientist from his earnest research with my invasive questions. Yet the wily poet was utterly without scruples in his rage to attain his goal. He felt he had chanced upon the most authentic source for discovering the secrets of the monkeys, and as luck would have it, the venerable Dr. Ervin—long loose scraggly white-haired and bushy silver-bearded— popped out of the woods. I swept forward to shake his hand, displayed a recent book of my poems and said I wanted to write an ode about the chimps. He greeted me warmly, and I promised my wife – still bristling with disdain – that I would take no more than a "few" minutes of his time. Once we began our exchange, he raced forward with amazing details of his research, and I jotted feverishly in my notepad for half an hour or so. He was convinced that the curious social network of the monkey clans exhibited traits of a depression-like illness that closely resembled clinical depression in humans. Dr. Ervin was an eminent psychiatrist from Montreal, hoping to learn new therapies for healing his hopelessly depressed patients.

PART IV

EXCERPTS FROM
THE POPE IN ST. LUCIA:
A TALE
OF THREE UNVEILINGS

by Laurence Lieberman

1.

As a child of thirteen,
it hurt his eyes to behold portraits
    of Saints and Angels—various heroes of legend and Bible
        lore—were peeling off the upper
            wall tier of Cathedral, just below
            the ceiling. Church-
        goers had complained for months,
                a whole year perhaps, that curlicues
        and flecks: thin shavings of dried paint,
    cracked silver-bits of color, were dropping into their hair.
Of late, the light hail
storm of paint scraps grew worse,
    becoming a thick mist of near-invisible motes when trade
            winds blew hardest. And children—
                looking up, while others pored over
            their prayer books—
        howled and whimpered. Pieces
                of indoors sky were falling, plummeting
        into their eyes . . .
                    For weeks, wild rumors
        flared: talk ran in the street—the church fathers planned
    to repair the portraits.
But who might they enlist to restore

those faded and crackling faces of Christ, Mary, Apostles
and the rest? Which artist, local
or foreign, would be summoned, then
brusquely appointed
to accomplish the great task? . . .
One sad Sunday, a common house painter
arrived unannounced in mid-service to set up
his stretch ladders and dropcloths. He climbed, step-tier by
tier, almost to the ceiling—
a standard paint bucket and wide hair
brushes in tow, then proceeded to plaster over the array
of ghostly haloed heads and winged
shoulders with enamel-thick erude
layers of cream-white
paint. Swipe by swipe, the rough
strokes of his brush blotted out
all those beatifio visages with gurgly
splatter sounds and echoings through the upper roof vaults
that rose above the voices
reciting liturgy, chapter and verse.
Dunstan recalls that he burst into tears. The cruellest
travesty he'd ever seen, those images
would haunt him and keep feeding
his powerful ambition
to become an artist in true service
of God and the Church . . .
Such memories,
distant but pained, came surging back
with a roar and flooded the grown man's early morning
work
revery, when first
it was announced in Spring '76
that the venerable Pope was planning a week-long visit

in just three months; whereupon
      he felt renewed horror and shame
    to fancy the Pope's
  eyes passing over blank lofty church
        wall expanse—where murals belonged.
In forty-nine-year-old mind's eye, fresh wall art was *a must*!
And though he'd won
some local fame as skilled muralist
  for his three-years-past grand floor-to-ceiling altar
      portrait in Roseau Church, Dunstan
        never dreamed *he* might be the one targeted
  for the noble mission.

2

In their early
teens, chums Derek and Dunstan nurtured
a mutual dream: to go
to Paris, live *from hand to mouth*
& learn their
trade. Both painters. They were wary about keeping
their identity pure . . .to resist
European masters of the past . . .to forge ahead
& make a bold new
Black islander's art. Free from White
culture's unholy grip.
No one in history,

Saint or Ikon,
was their superior. But they singled
out favorites. . . . Dunstan's
imported hi-fi turntable, perhaps
the first, ever,
in St. Lucia, regaled them
endlessly, to Mozart and Beethoven,
and plied their brushes—easels propped in tandem
upon a forgotten
old nook in tower ruins of the former
Ministry of Culture
(cannons, dislodged

from their mounts,
stood upright in corners: mossy relics
of the old French Fort) . . .
They relished the great vista over-
look of seashore

& Pitons' conic hilltops. They boosted each other's
        works, praising this *lad's* magic lines,
that *mate's* gut-wrenching colors, and crowed over
being *Top Dogs*
        of the Castle. Play, more and more, felt
        like a half step, a quarter
step, from soaring

           to the Sublime.
        Which did not prepare them for the pained
shock of roaring genius—
        their first glimpse of sublimities
actualized! . . .
Color plates of Michelangelo's fierce-eyed portraits
        from the Sistine Chapel, viewed in an art
portfolio book checked out on Antilles inter-library
loan, were seared
        forever into memory—like touch of white hot
        coals to their fingertips.
How emboldening,

           those first peeps
        at the uncanny lifelike prints staring back
into their eyes with orbs
        more blazing than anyone's piercingly
real eyes. To see
it, once-and-for-all-time, was to be changed utterly.
        To know that the superhuman space lurks
in every Soul, waiting for *The Few* to take command
& swiftly channel
        its energies . . . Boys they were, of no more
        than fifteen years! But Dunstan
would never forget

                how they threw
            their arms around old pillars, stone columns
        luckily still in place,
            though portions of the three-story-high
        roof they supported
        were fallen, or blown away by hurricanes. The Maestro's
            paint faces shook them so hard, they lost
    their balance—held on for dear life, no telling if
    they might be hurled
            over upper story porch railings to sudden
            deaths on the coastal rocks
below . . . They hugged

                slanting pillars
            to their breasts, wailing for terror and joy
        mixed. What was the source
            of all that shattering energy—power
        surging out at them
        from the painted figures like an earthquake? Or perhaps
            something in their own adolescent quaking
    frames, willowy tall thin physiques, was tearing them
    apart as they froze
            stock still and clasped those stanchions
            of stone. It spoke to them, in
a language they knew

from another
life—a strange tongue they were apprised of,
from birth. What they heard,
little guessing it at the time, was
their own Souls' voice
echoing, sighing in sync. Until that day, they'd always
supposed art *Mission*, the *Calling*, was half
play, half juvenile wish fantasy. But they were already
spoken for. *The Chosen* . . .
Half-blinded, they both grew dizzy at once.
It was the most intense vertigo
they'd ever known.

3.

Three or four befuddled committees, who were distraught and combative
         by turns, threw up their hands.
      On one choice, only, could they agree—to seek Dunstan's
         help, to summon *him* to the rescue. *Why me?*,
      he didn't ask them aloud. But answered, communing with his inner ear.
               Nobody else
         could throw himself into painting such a huge wall
            surface (*three hundred square*
                  meters, mon!:
               the size of a modern football
            field), do the job as fast, or for so little pay.
               Surely it seemed
      impossible for anyone to beautify those church walls quickly enough
         to be in time for the Pope's visit, just three
      months off. But the word *impossible* would draw his best work
            from him, as it always had
done before. His one condition they happily agreed to. His four sons,

                           all budding artists,
                     must be granted full license
                  to work in tandem with their father . . .
                  That whole first week would be allotted
               to repair wall plasters and refurbish the drab church
                     interior—the *puny* scarred baptismal
                           fount, to begin,
                     must be overhauled and varnished.
                  They'd hire out a crew of masons, carpenters,
                           for the nuts-
               and-bolts hard labor, blue collar tasks. But Dunstan
                  won unconditional *clout* to supervise all
                     their efforts . . . Breathing space!
                           The reprieve week—

swinging of hammers, brick-laying and pouring concrete—bought him
time to gird up his courage
to face the permanent multi-mural layout of the people's
number one sanctuary of faith: the Cathedral
of Castries itself. *When that whole linked chain of fourteen murals
is finished,*
he told himself, *I'll make even Michelangelo look
small.* He'd give all those Church
Art Masters
before him *a run for their money!*
As his grand plan took shape, he knew he dare not
divulge to the High
Parish elders how totally he meant to break with tradition and strike
out for his new concept. A rebel to the core,
he was. But only his team of partner sons would know the ruse
in advance, sly revolution
their sire concocted. All turn-of-the-century paintings on upper walls

and ceiling—bland
faces garishly painted over,
but he recalled them from his childhood
years—were dour formula portraits of Saints,
Divinities, Angels and Apostles: the epitome of White
French colonial art. No trace of native
or indigenous
folk life. Still less true ikons
of the common people. He would burn down long-
dead legend
faces of France, and resurrect them as St. Lucia's own
local men, ladies and children. Not just home-
land types. That would be heresy
enough to call

down the wrath of most High Clerics and Deacons. But he meant to go
that native route *one better*
and paint some eccentric townsfolk: unique private
citizens, giving them public grandeur—
as well as perpetuity—in his new suite of murals. He would put off,
or postpone
for as long as possible, the fierce revelation:
portraits were to be likenesses—
if mildly
disguised—of his actual living
friends and neighbors. In many face drafts, both he
and his helpmate sons
took care to leave out a few key salient features (big giveaway hook
nose, pronounced chin dimple, telltale deformed
eye pouch, riven ear lobe, cheek or forehead cicatrix: battle
scars of a famed knife bout),
until the last stage of portraiture—to hold at bay those many casual

observers strolling
through the church and prone to peer
at wall art. They were determined to let
no one guess who might be living prototypes
for particular visages, demeanors—and thus to deflect
any rumors brewing that the artists
secretly employed
local models at all . . . Dunstan's
working principle, here, sprang from his sudden
breakthrough
idea. All the Saints must once have been deeply flawed
humans, mere flesh-and-blood folks like our-
selves. And who is to say, this one,
not that one,

shall be eligible for painterly canonization in oils, gouaches, dyes
          or acrylics? . . . Your artist
     maker, Dunstan or whoever, need only find himself working
          at such a pitch and elevated state as to gain
     faith that he has inexplicably become the crude vessel through which
          God's own *WILL*
          may be articulated: the vulgar sinful muralist, thereby,
               lifted into a realm wherein
                    his work serves
                    as the Medium for Divinity.
     By instinct, then, the maker of murals ever shall know
               he *must* happen
     upon—by Fate, not accident—the right local faces to be alchemized,
          as if overnight, into Sainthood . . . Often,
     to distract too-clever watchers, churchgoers who hung around
          for hours, peeping over shoulders
of the artist-in-motion, balancing ever higher on his extended ladders,

                              his son assists
                         would scurry about and apply
                         themselves to body-wrenching tasks
                         of moving heavy floor blocks to one side
                    or another. In his zeal for repositioning church zones,
                         even inventing new seats of Holy
                              Hour enactment,
                         he added two new *thrones* between
                    rows of pews, near front and center—a high
                                   tabernacle
                    grooved into one wall panel, a larger baptismal fount
                         installed in a more prominent central
                              aisle. *See it here*, he says.
                                   It's now big

enough for someone of bulk to take a bath in it. Before, it was just
a little dinky fountain
catcher by the side door . . . Hence, suspicions of nosey
lookers-on were allayed till the final week
before public unveiling of the finished commission—barely two days
prior to the Pope's
visit. Long past the point of no return, if outraged
church dignitary were to issue
a protest,
or try to inveigle that family
team of artists to change course . . . And what a surprise—
to the whole throng
assembled—it was! All ethnic breeds, denominations, Races of dear
beauteous St. Lucia were included. The spirit
of the portraits was to embrace all peoples, equally: Hindus,
Jews, Protestants, Africans,
East Indians, indigenous Caribs . . . At the unveiling, church overseers

held a Low Mass:
St. Omer presented a brief
lecture declaring his *Manifesto*
answering to expected charges. A *Rebel*,
to be sure. But no *Libertine*. No shameless *Profligate* . . .
In his defense, he made an eloquent
plea directly
to attendant flock of commoners
(those wrangling committees, after all, had
dropped the whole
package in the artist's lap); but to begin, he lavished
high praise upon his four gifted sons.
Without their indispensable
helps, no way

could he otherwise have met the early deadline. Then he singled out
        Luici, his eldest, and best
    art teacher in St. Mary's College, whose twenty foremost
        students had leant a helping hand: comings
    & goings to replenish supplies, and climbing into those wall alcoves
        less accessible
    to six-and-a-half-foot Dunstan and the very tall clan
        of St. Omer males. But impresario
            for the whole
        project—at every stage—was,
        unfailingly, the artist himself . . . He would interrupt
            his discourse, at
    intervals, to take questions from the gallery—so many folks packed
        together for the occasion, some few rows
    of overflow watchers trailing outside into the adjacent
        gardens, while many strained
to hear above the hubbub. How does he find the energy and fortitude

                        to work so fast,
                    and for such long hours, with no
                loss of that superior draughtsmanship
                in every detail? In reply, he postulates his
            direct pipeline to God. While his artist cronies & peers
                often turn to Buddhism, of late, to tap
                    into great source
                of *transpersonal Being*—he finds
            he can never forsake personal desire, nor will
                    relinquish
        blind heat of passion. The *Incarnation* is the great core
                of his Christian faith. Unswerving.
                    Unshakable, that direct
                        one-on-one

meeting of man and the Lord is everything to him. (Usually, he vows
he's committed to withhold
secrets of his new-found craft and art theory. But in church,
today, why not spell out to the askers
his formula of spiritual bent?) . . . His system, without fail. Meditate
for three hours—
from six to nine each morning—and give your will, utterly,
to God. Thus he freed of private
ego. Or
ambition. Then, always, *The Man*
reciprocates. And whenever Dunstan attains that instant
of being freed
of will—an exact pinpointed moment in time—God renews and
quadruples
his energies. Only then can he throw himself
totally into the wall mural, without recourse to a plan or least
premeditated design . . . And how
does he come by his vast unflagging strength? *Ah, I'm so terribly strong*

because I destroy
my own will every day to build
pure vacancy wherein God's Will may work
its magic in me. Then I become an impersonal
medium through which He can pass, unimpeded . . . In the next
breath, he digresses to musically chant
his *Self Prayers,*
that litany of commands normally
uttered to his dark ethereal demon whenever
his brushes speed
forward too hastily for his mind controls. *Curb ego. Pull*
back. All that you paint in the people's church
must serve to fortify their frail
spirits to ascend.

5.

In a flash
it came to him . . . Sparkly mode.
Glittering structure that would fit
all fragments of his mural into a single
grand theme. He sought one pure emblem to link up
the widest array of portraits.
When he found
it, the image shook him,
gave him a cycle of fierce trembles
and shudders—
an invasive supernatural typhoon of Being. He knew
that airborne symbol must be vouchsafed
to him by Divinity . . . A capacious
dazzling cup

floated over his head and offered
    itself up to him,
        as in a hallucination. Or waking
            dream. He extended
his hand to touch it, but his fingers passed through,
in one side and out the other. Yet the glass

                would continue
            to look as firm and substantial
        as a metal goblet. Many distinct gem-
    like nuggets embedded in the rim sparkled
and glimmered. They seemed to emit their own light.
This bowl-shaped vessel, many-
            faceted, hung
        suspended above his brow.

He kept trying to reach for the wide cup,
to take it
in his hand, lift it to his lips and heartily quaff
its contents. Perhaps it contained some
elixir, a healing potion . . .
But at last

he came to see it was the mere shape
of an idea—a sweet
gift of thought, embodied in a palpable
image. *Jewels*
in a Chalice. That emblem would weave together all
circumambient diverse parts of his mural.

Fourteen oval
portraits. Fourteen separate
stations, one to represent each town-
ship or municipality of his whole country.
Every rounded picture would be graced with a couple
of actual living citizens
from each locale,
decked out in their own true
modern clothes. Those homey familiar
faces would be
mixed, randomly, with notable heroes of worldwide
renown—the *Ugandan Martyrs,* for one.
A local man and woman, as
by disguise,

might be blent into each composite.
A daring move, scary
and innovatory, he would be the first church
artist to import
mostly Black Ikons into the formerly White Christian
array of saints, once-mortal time travellers

now mingled
with today's flesh-and-blood
sinners. The chalice format would best
enable the townsfolk to take in that whole
linked succession of fourteen intertwined portrait
murals, at a glance. Over time,
while circling
the church interior, repeatedly,
all beholders would come to see that each
distinct oval
painting belonged—by adjacent overlappings—to one
irreducible design. As they studied
the unique oval layouts,
ambling past,

Dunstan's dream of many jewels rimming
a single Eucharistic
Cup would bewitch them: a vision of unity
coming, at last,
to each regular church-goer. First drawing his viewers
into those deep-set story scenes, one by one,

He'd allure them
to espouse each narrative
grouping of familial and historic
folks, before giving any thought to webwork
encompassing them all. The mini-murals would thrive
as distinct vivid portraits first,
each making its
own poignant claim on the lookers'
affections. Inset of the *Roundels* in deep
wall recess,
or window niche, should enhance the gradual two-step
process of grasping the full wraparound
mural linkage as unified
aggregate

rondure. This first replacement of olden
colonial church faces
with Black Ikons, he prayed, might dispel last
manacles of slavery—
returning the foremost House of Worship to the common
folks . . . A true People's Palace for the future.

6.

As in Martinique and urban
Guadeloupe, churches in St. Lucia
were designed by French architects for colonial French
congregations: French-
speaking, French-dressing White folks
at prayer . . . His passion was to transform all
local churches
into true indigenous castles for God
and his Host. Each, a people's
temple for today, starting with the Cathedral of Castries
and then working on down
to all lesser village parish
houses, no matter how small . . . First step.
They would replace

Latin in hymnals and prayer-
texts with the local vernacular.
Second step. A bigger jump, harder. Takes much longer.
To replace White Christ,
White Ikons, White God with their Black
counterparts. This goal, Dunstan was the earliest
to accomplish
on a pervasive scale in St. Lucia's
High Cathedral. Down to lowly
apostles and the lesser angels—all Black portraits would
supplant the Whites . . . Thus,
he expounded his brave aesthetic
at the opening Mass for his multi-mural
unveiling: *I'm*

a propagandist, he declared.
"I must be. How else might I paint
with fire in my veins, raw fervor in my heart? I work
for the sure coming
ascendancy of the Black man and woman
on the planet. And it all starts in your home
ground. Therefore,
I'm an optimist. And I believe in
historical determinism. The Blacks
are overdue for a great rebound in world affairs. My murals
will always promulgate
my Black Theology. These wall
portraits are all dedicated to that *Advent.*
New better life

for our Black Race, world-
wide. My noblest task is to work
for our enhancement on the world stage, but at highest
spirit levels—never
to the exclusion of other Races.
That toughest lesson I would hope to teach
with bold murals—
if your God is of a different Race
you will always be fettered. In
shackles. Forever a slave. In Church Art, the great mission
and privilege, today,
is ever to perpetuate your own
differences: of Race, of faith, of homeland . . ."
All this discourse

was eloquently spoken, once
more, for the silk-robed Pope's ears
at the second unveiling, days later. And with the Pope

as witness, he took
the further plunge of chanting his own
improvised psalm, a self-hymn, whatever the risk
of being spurned
as arrogant: *A MAN WALKED THE FACE*
OF THE EARTH . . . HE WAS A GOD . . .
SO YOU ARE A GOD . . . BUT FOR MODESTY'S SAKE,
YOU DO NOT SAY

YOU ARE A GOD . . . SO YOU
SAY YOU ARE SON OF GOD . . . AND BLACK . . .
AND GOD The Pope kept slowly walking, drawing
his silken train

along the floor behind him,
surveying the fourteen brilliant
Roundels, each sunk in its shallow niche of church wall.
And with his keen eyes
aglow, he marvelled at the beauty
of style, never doubting that all fourteen stations—
if peopled with
some actual resident Blacks commingled
in the family of Saints & Angels—
purely served the Holy Spirit. Nor did his Eminence, by word
or glance, seem to take
umbrage at the word bouquet so boldly
recited—since Dunstan's verse refrain and pictorial
scenes blossomed

a common message, his words
and images mated at every turn
of the Pope's circling ambles. Any chagrin he'd felt
was kept under wraps,
muffled by his final litany

of praise. The murals had enthralled him, capti-
vated his heart . . .
The artist trembled, melted in tears
from relief—for he'd taken
the gamble of tying a secular knot between Church and Island
State. He pled his case,
St. Lucia is . . . The Church is . . . Entities
inviolate. If you believe in them, you must preserve
both, interfused.

12

To Dunstan, poetry is the unrivalled
Queen of the Arts. The Word reigns supreme in his lexicon
    of life and art. Everything
            originates from the Word, and Dame Poetry
is the lifeblood and shrine of words. Since he and his soul mate
           Derek nurtured each other's first
fruits, the painter *campadre*
    had a lightning-quick grasp of Derek's
      verse. No surprise, then, the just-completed

      manuscript of *Omerus* was secretly
entrusted to Dunstan. He pored over the work, giving up
    every inch of his Being
        to the read for five days. And he basked
in its power to give a shape to their shared boyhood and youth,
        then returned the bound raggedy
pages to his friend, saying—
    I can give you absolution right now . . .
    This book had to be the perfect culmination

    of the poet's life in a *Confessional*
Odyssey. You are now absolved of all your sins, and freed
    from your least misgivings of past
      failure . . . So it seemed natural for him
to turn to Derek for succor, when he commenced that first brief
      holiday from Fort-de-France to face
down his worst spirit crisis
    at home. He was stricken—as never before—
      with doubts about the possible false currency

of words in the Bible. For Scripture had
grown increasingly suspect to him, of late: how do we know
　　those words of chapter and verse
　　　　　are not counterfeit, mere shoddy forgeries—
if we consider that men who penned the holy verses were *fumbling*
　　　　　blockheads, puny oafish mortals
like ourselves? Ultimately,
　　the whole thing should be a disaster,
　　　　he said—throwing himself upon the indulgent

　　mercy of his friend the poet, caretaker
of Words, sacred and profane alike. For years, he'd put all
　　doubts behind him. Or eluded
　　　　his sceptic bent by taking crude solace
from a reckless credo: *I might as well gamble everything on God's*
　　　　　holy tutelage. For without my
great faith, I'd just commit
　　suicide . . . But in the grips of his most
　　　　awesome task and burden, ever, in Martinique

　　this paltry mantra no longer sufficed.
He felt immense terror, let he desecrate the *People's Citadel*—
　　that noblest House of Worship—
　　　　by slathering his most sensuous bold color
palette on the linked chain of murals *in bad faith.* And everyone who
　　　　viewed the finished work assuredly
would be able to detect
　　its maker's glum shakiness of spirit
　　　　in every decorative glamor or nicety of paint

style, no matter how much cosmetic
beauty he could muster to hide the spirit void at the core.
    So how can mere flawed humans
        like you and me set about to accurately
transcribe the words of God? We're not fit to be God's stenographers.
        No way . . . Derek's reply, a plain-
spoken and simple adage.
    My trade is metaphor. And he paused,
        while his muralist comrade struggled to catch

    his drift. *But man himself is finite,*
so no man can write The Truth. Though for inspired moments
        he may seem to approximate
            truth, he must fail—since any man, woman
or child who reads the Scriptures will be forced to view the fables
            in their own privately evolved
mind light, and to translate
        sacred words into their ego-flawed
            lingos. Hence the many contradictory gleanings

    of Bible lore, as varied as the vast
number of readers. Or hearkeners to church service. Again,
    great messages, never directly
        given, must be mirrored in legends, myths,
fables. *If we stare at God's light directly, it shall sear our eyes*
            and blind us. Dunstan, don't forget
that Christ says—Call no man
    teacher. The one teacher is the Holy
        Spirit . . . By a kind of magic, ordinary people

131

wrote Scripture, but they were acting
as crude vehicles through which God's light may pass. What
     saves the Bible is metaphor,
                    Holy Spirit lifting the literal stories
into double seeing. A second sight. Meaning has always come to us
                    by such roundabout turns and twists.
Loftiest speech or written
     verbiage, if raised to exalted pitch,
          must work as metaphor . . . *The Bible is poetry.*

     Derek sent him back to Fort-de-France
armed with new faith in word magic, but left him on the ropes
     in his struggles with the Devil
               (the verse master, himself, entertained
some qualms, but couldn't dismiss the Fiend outright—for he
harbored
               demonic impulse in his own soul) . . .
Ongoing work at murals
     would be Dunstan's arena for thrashing
          Satan: walls of St. Michael's, the battleground.

13.

The first day back to his ladders & scaffolds, he takes fire
                                    from all his new resolves.
    For three hours, he gives the biggest part
of himself to God. As before, he wins his way to *that space.*

                    Total well-
            being. Soon he is able to get free. Then,
                    before he paints
        a single stroke, he rehearses his foremost
    mantras for buoying his spirit. First, he must never
            forgo his great passion
        to propogate the Black Christ in his art, and
            thereby bulwark his Dark
        Race's promise for the future. Worldwide.
            Today, I'm so terribly
    strong, for I've destroyed my own will to let God's Will

be working in me. Thus, I know I cannot fail . . . Nobody else
                                believes as hugely as I do
        when I come to emblazon my murals! But then,
the hostile church walls seem to push back, even hurl away,

                    his softest
            brush strokes. And he launches into a spiel.
                Fierce soliloquy.
        His debating form has never been more trenchant.
    He clings to his hard-bought inner security and spouts
            terms of his ongoing
    wrangle with the Church, both home & abroad. He'd
            always be an *innovator,*
            but no *heretic.* Hence, he remains irre-

trievably *in the fold.* . . .
Now his strokes are coming unfettered, more free-and-easy

as the wall obstruction starts to fall away. He's puffing
and his tall ladder sways
with his vehemence. No way will he relent,
much less fall. His voice grows strident, for he proclaims—

Never again
shall I endure any timid church pieties,
lame drabness or
pettiness of spirit. He insists on blazing
into his fullest happiness at work, every day. Such
discipline of loving
gusto, of verve, he puts above his art. Puts
Love above the churchly
Law. These are his best weapons against
Satan, whom he still deems
to be *a fraud.* A mainstay, these tenets of his philosophy

effervescing on the fly. His ideas come tumbling forth as he
drafts—with broadest arm
sweeps—outlines of three celestial figures
in a fresh wall mural. Next, as he carefully picks his colors,

he may take
comfort, anew, from his empirical schema-
tics of *Prismism.*
Bold solid whole colors. That's all he needs.
An instrument that will allow him to articulate his
most complex agendas.
The sheer simplicity of both palette and line-
work owes no small debt

to his study of Matisse; for this, he's
quick to give due credit.
But he's ever wary about paying tribute to *The Moderns*

since he competes only with Michelangelo and Diego Rivera—
no other muralists even
need be reckoned with as true rivals.
He snickers, to think of the decline in the art of painting

after Michel-
angelo: how all large-scale works fell off,
deteriorating into
Baroque and Rococo. Oh yes, the Master's heirs
achieve perfection, of sorts. But the word Artist—
as applied to them—should
not be murmured in the same breath . . . A rotund
priest enters the chapel
as he muddles through this heated one-man
debate. He hushes up!
Sucks down his embarrassment. But maintains his willowy

buoyant demeanor as he paints. And won't let any tremor
of apology flit across
his features to quench the cleric's tacit
rebuke to his babbles—peppered with a string of expletives . . .

What a relief!
Portly churchman dashes out the side exit
rather than challenge
the muralist's tart and profane tonguings. No
power on earth would compel him to kiss the priest's
ass. Perhaps he'd lick
God's ass—nobody else's. How well he knows

that sort of sycophancy
will kill a man's talent very fast.
Or, at best, his work
assuredly must wither in a few years . . . During the first

hours since his return, he boosts his nerve with many such
oratorical and cerebral
gambits. By midday, he's flying high, while
the walls relent. They don't resist his relaxed *or* fiery moves,

his undulant
sweet arm swings. Then, by a sudden impulse—
surprising himself—
he shifts his ladder back to the crucial half-
finished scene of St. Michael subduing that hellish
demon, and takes a few brave
swipes at the prostrate grovelling Lucifer . . .
But then his arm yanks
back, aghast at a return of his doubts.
If you are what they say
you are, God must not be omnipotent. Why would God create

the Devil? . . . His pause, he knows, is but momentary lapse
to regroup and better
mobilize his supreme moves. Nothing less
than his best will suffice, today of all days. Now he finds

he is idly
humming tunes from Mozart's *Requiem*, arias
from *The Magic*
Flute—catching himself in the act! For letting
those song motifs gently rumble in his throat and go
lolloping through his brain

136

is a diversion from the stress of his anguish.
Or process of self-
healing that may spring up, unwilled surge,
from the killing silence.
And as he takes command of this medley of voices and song

notes tossed haphazardly over his tongue and larynx, he's
reminded of the ardor
he'd always found in the mind-balm of music.
His great love of melody, he now discerns, is mysteriously

linked to his
love of numbers. He's never been so happy
as when at play
with math sums, toying with sets of variables
as he plotted his simplest drawings and difficult
murals, alike. He follows
out this line of thinking and then discovers
in his raw secret
mind that just as music naturally spills
over into number games,
soon the quiet relaxed joys of math hatch into juggling

of colors in his work with paint, and that flux of color
hues generates ideas.
Fantasy. But now he sees—as never before—
in the workings of imagination at play, how underpinnings

of his broad-
scale art were always bound up with song,
math and philosophy.
And then he takes the leap that may save him
in his wrestling bouts with Satan. *O what do we know,*

beyond doubt?, he asks
himself—while still nursing his gravest doubts.
Only two truths are handed
to us in absolute. We are born. And we
shall die. Our life term
is finite, and we humans tend to view each other and our

world only in finite terms. That is our limited range—
                                        the finite dimension . . .
But Derek has given him *metaphor*, which
expands, or layers, our vision. Doublings, without limit.

On the verge
of one last insight he needs, much as man
dying of thirst
craves a drink, he suddenly recalls the great
pleasure he'd taken in Binary Math. A route for mind
to throw off the shackles,
the limits of finitude. Binary seeing holds that
all things must have
an opposite. A coin cannot exist without
two sides. Our planet
rotates on two poles. Everyone lives and dies someplace

between the two. One is needed to balance the other. And
                                        therefore, Satan must
be the opposite side of God. Either one
proves—guarantees—the reality of the other. By some bold

leap of faith,
we can trust this odd marriage of polarities . . .
All at once, he feels
He's out of the woods. His fabulous new tool—

Prismism—is binary to the core. These murals, then,
fourteen grand facets
spread over five walls and juxtaposed panels,
shall be his first assay
in the mode of purely prismatic color
works. Any rift, or schism,
between opposites can be resolved by nimble maneuverings

of color. Color likes, color repulsings, side-by-side in
adjacent murals, would
convey holy or irreverant messages. Wisdom,
over and above the story. The reconciling of color extremes,

such findings
of harmony, would evoke the Holy Spirit.
Like Van Gogh's un-
earthly sunflower light, lordly Spirit would
come charging out at viewers of his murals from sheer
power of color contrasts.
There's the secret of the Devil—held in check,
bound by the artist's
control of warring shades, lights and darks.
By wielding such color
power, nothing would seem impossible for him, all problems

solved. The light of the Holy Spirit would flutter and
bleed through gyrations
of color tints, color hues, no jot less
pungently than by tumultuous images of a novelist or poet.

In religion,
    he would assuage
        all problems with joy.
        And resolve all
struggle with happy spirit. Now that
was the ticket. The key for his Soul to prevail.
        In art, he'd chasten
        those many irreconcilables

with diversity
    of color. Only
        if his power with hue con-
        trasts be strong
enough, brilliant and overpowering
to the viewers, might he hope to deliver them
        from worst racial
        stereotypes. They could take

comfort in his
    black Christ, black
        Mary, those black apostles
        and ink-black
St. Michael. Ah, he'd long nurtured
a penchant to make color range in his portraits
        be bold enough
        to convey any message. Now,

at last, he felt
   ready to put his
      new-minted rainbow strategy
      to a first test.
Prismism, he named it. Slow in coming
to fruition, his earliest attempts to formulate
       this ideal work
       mode dated back to his years

of drafting swift
   bright water colors,
      oils and pen-and-ink sketches,
      most dashed off
by the score as he worked side by side
with his rival and Brother in the Spirit, Derek:
      the budding Poet
      Laureate hid in coming-of-age

painter. His Soul
   Mate chose Cubism
      as preferred modern genre, while
      Dunstan dabbled
in Cubism, too, for a time. He explored
a few strategems, but gave it up. Too intellectual
      and abstract for
      his growing hypnotic color

bias . . . In Martinique,
    to distract priests
        and flocks of French parishioners
        from their narrow
politics of skin shades, the paint dance
of epidermal tints, he'd set out to captivate them
            with a sensuous
                blaze of color contrasts. Disarm

minds of bigotry—
    Polemics of Race—
        with color speech, messages that
        work their way
like flung javelins of light from eye's
trance to mindscape. *Prismism* . . . Art sorcerer, he'd
            preach with that wand—
            his brush of pigments, as a poet

charms and instructs
    numberless readers
        with magical words and phrases.
        He sought to make
rapt statements, to articulate his ideas—
by the way color behaves. To ravish hearts, bewitch
            spirits, with surprise
            color variants—those generated

by prisms catching,
     filtering & bending
          the light. All prism shades
          may be derived
from three whole colors: red, yellow, blue . . .
Color trinity that can yield whatever blends might
               be needed to win
               lax hate-filled minds sweetly away

from color-blind
     mental bedevilments.
          From that tawdry brain circus
          of Black and White
swept away, swept finally away. Blacks,
all prism colors heaped together. Whites, a total
               absence of color.
               Ah, he would bedazzle the eye

and inveigle souls
     with the great play
          of whole primary colors safely
          gamboling between
those poles, and thereby usurp attention
away from the deadly end zones. A rainbow dazzle over-
               powering White & Black
               Races . . . Murderous antipodes.

Often before, noted
    authors had passed through Castries,
wishing to write his bio . . .
    He'd put them off, saying—"My life
is not about a series
    of dates, events, occasions. Only *I*
know what I was doing.
    My life's always been a pursuit
of some ancient dream.
    A search. So I do not let those
transient comers lay blunt
    hands upon it . . . They may not touch
very quick of my source—
    always unfolding, my life's not
even in my own grasp.
But I've gleaned, if you should happen
to find great beauty
    in life, you can't keep it to yourself
alone. It's a command
    from God. All beauty must be shared
with others . . . And nobody
    loves life more than I do, I love
every inch of it. But I
    also confess to a towering conceit,
my pride in my Black Genes—
    yes, my legacy of Race. That's it.
It will not let me accept
    that anyone else is better than me.
No one alive today,
    no man or woman who came before,
no forerunner . . ."

Five years
   after completing his Martinique
commission, he visited
   the Tate Gallery in South London,
and he found himself
   unexpectedly engaged in a two-way
dispute with Rembrandt's
   Self-portrait. Ah, they spoke by turns,
time and time again—
   every word tinged with the nuance
of mutual respect . . .
   The debate grew heated at the finish,
but all the while they
   spoke, he knew they were having a love
wrangle between equals.
   No winner or loser. No rivalry, or
juggling for high rank.
   Love moved freely both ways—the fragile
threshold between alive
   and dead fell away. Vanished. Just
two equals conversing
   under God . . .
      I don't make heroes out of
anybody, he says.
   But if asked to choose the one artist
he holds in highest
   esteem, Van Gogh is the one. Last week,
when he came upon
   Van Gogh's *Sunflower* works in a museum
exhibit, he was stunned—
   taken by surprise, for he'd studied
those paintings in art
   books, and he felt they'd already grown

as familiar to his glance
    as his own best creations. But no,
the mint canvases seemed
    totally foreign to his eyes and mind.
Unknown. And impossible
    to believe! He kept looking for flood-
lights on the floor,
    or hidden in the ceiling overhead,
hurling such unruly
    glare upon the portraits. And it crossed
his mind to wheedle
    security guards to soften the intense
beams, and let those
    masterworks be bathed only in natural
light. It was a disgrace
    for them to try to enhance genius with
paltry artificial
    rays. And he was at the point of saying—
let the works speak
    for themselves, when he was overcome
with terror . . .
        By impulse
    ungovernable, he covered both eyes with
his hands, then slowly
    peeled back his fingers, one by one,
to give his tardy
    eye muscles time to adjust to new scale
of brightness. Mere oil
    on canvas discharged flashes that seemed
powerful enough to blind
    a viewer. Inner light—the light of Souls!—
had been embodied
    in paint, given a palpable form, as never

146

before. *Ha, Witchcraft*
it must be! Or Demon possessed. Thereupon
he learned that God's
radiance and Satan's could seem identical.
You could mistake
one for the other, except for Love ablaze,
generated solely
by the first . . . Pure joy of heart, shaped &
conveyed with torrid
color & line. *Thank God I'm alive,* the gold
Sunflowers exclaim.

THE POET ON THE POEM

"The Pope in St. Lucia"

Returning from Guyana, I booked a last-minute stop-off for a few days in St. Lucia, my first visit to the island in 13 years. I rented a room in a guest-house near the airport, dropped off my bags, and began walking into down-town Castries. . . . Small quaint bookstore. I ask the manager if she knows whether Dunstan St. Omer is in town. She smiles. *Midday, he's always at the Cathedral. A very tall man. Probably seated next to a pretty woman* . . . Short walk to church. As I enter, he pops up in a distant front pew, laughs, murmurs *Can that be you? Yes,* I salute. Reunion unfolds. Alas, he never received the book I mailed to him, *The Mural of Wakeful Sleep,* titled after my poems in response to his fabulous early church mural and stained-glass windows. Belatedly, I place a copy in his hand. (Those poems first appeared in *APR* in 1985.)

Next morning at breakfast, Dunstan proposes that I embark on a fuller verse—communing with his art—a *partnership* he calls it. Several days of interviews follow. We drive to various local sites to give me an updated survey of works—mostly murals—which I hadn't viewed before. Later, he treats me to a perusal of many vibrant slides of paintings he'd been commissioned to produce for other islands, most notably his block of murals for the new Church of St. Christopher in Fort-du-France. Acclaimed the highest honor of his career! He dwells at some length on the near-impossible demands of that Martinique project. When we return to the Cathedral in Castries, he recounts the joys and trials of his dizzyingly rushed three months of fashioning this cycle of fourteen murals in time for the Pope's anticipated first visit to St. Lucia.

More than ever before, I find myself inwardly questioning my meager resources, and I start to quail before the exacting task I appear to have impulsively undertaken. I'm strictly an outsider in this island milieu, which puts me at a first grim remove; and my access to the events my host generously shares with me is hopelessly secondhand, which greatly widens the gulf I cannot reasonably hope to traverse . . . But as Dunstan slips into a reverie about the *indispensable* help his four gifted sons gave him with the final murals for the Cathedral, I'm swept back thirteen years to the day his four boys fitted sister Digna into the amazing bulky garment they crafted for her song-and-dance medley in the Miss St. Lucia contest. I watched, breathless, as they lowered the lovely multi-tiered costume from the garage rafters onto her frail trembling shoulders. And it was I who finally drove her in my rental Datsun—she teasing me all the while for my nervous stutter— to the vast banana shed stadium where she would be crowned Island Queen late that night. During those weeks, I came to be welcomed as an adoptive son of the St. Omer family. And for today's reunion, perhaps I become—once again—a familial honoree. . . .

Often, I recall with gratitude my chance first meeting with Derek Walcott at the Guggenheim Museum one night in 1980, just two weeks prior to my scheduled flight to St. Lucia for a lengthy stay. He kindly suggested that I must be sure to *ring up* his best friend Dunstan at the start of my visit. Soon I would learn that the two soul mates—as teenagers—were inseparable buddy painters. For Derek, poetry would come later . . . My second visit was in 1993. Walcott had won the Nobel Prize the year before for his poem *Omeros*. Dunstan took relish in telling me that he was the first, ever, to read his pal's manuscript, and he reported to Derek on the spot—*I can give you absolution now.*

My long poem "The Pope in St. Lucia" was beset by many false starts, at intervals of two or three years. Those several drafts were all pen-written, and later versions were reworked on a manual typewriter—never a computer. When the last first draft took hold, I had no idea whether I was engaged in a single long poem or a linked sequence of shorter works. Most of my long poems have passed through a similar uncertain incubation. Normally, I gravitate to a mode of shorter self-contained units, and I may not discover if the extended manuscript will come together as a cohesive whole until a very late stage of revising. My early drafts are usually formless. I don't begin to explore patterns of line and stanza until I sense that I have a completed—or fully amplified—version in hand. This intermediate phase of my work predisposes me to feel a certain comfort with magazine publication of a few excerpts from the full composition . . . As now.

EXODUS OF BUTTERFLIES

One whole afternoon, Franz and his protege
    Winfred sat on freshly hewn tree stumps, and brooded
together over the great five-hundred-year-old
    holy tree leaning over Franz's boyhood home. He'd come to love
    that huge black sage tree like a grand old uncle
        who'd grown ever more crusty
          and mellow with age. But the tree's gnarled roots
        had punctured the main sewage pipes
          of the town, then tore
            wide cracks across the road like an earthquake.
          So despite protests of nearby

home owners, the city fathers voted
        to cut her down in just three days. Chagrined Franz
wept at the prospect, and regaled Winfred
    with tales of family nurtured by the lordly tree. His young
friend
    promised he would muster a series of paintings
        to honor the blessed tree's
          spirit—to that end, he mused upon its densely
    outblown expanse of limbs and branches.
        He stayed and stayed, long
          after Franz retired for bed, holding steady
          in his brooding eye sharp images

of the tree by twilight, fullmoon light,
        starlight, and morning sun. Then he caught and held
vivid moments of the wind-blown tree in sudden
    gusts, wet tree drenched with five-minute downpours of rain,
calm
       tree in dry still hours. His sketchbook in hand,
        he was growing familiar
           with the tree's wide mood swings. Her gaiety. Her
       sulkiness. Her cringing at putrid smokes
        and whirling gas fumes
           from too many passing cars. Her welcome embrace
           of whole schools of nesting birds—

she loved nothing better than to be weighed
        down by great scads of birthing gulls. In last hours
before the chain saws came to gnaw and slice
    through her centuries-thick tiers and layers of rings, he savored
    her fulsome girth, from bark to bole . . . The night
       after she was razed
           to a wide low stump, Winfred dreamed that he sleeps
       beside the fallen tree and awakes to find
         the long zipper running
           across his abdomen has burst open, releasing
           a stream of twenty-two butterflies

(varicolored, and of many wing designs)
       from the long slit in his belly. In the wild dream
he struggles to pull the flaps of his gaping
    wound back together, but whenever he tugs those flaps of flesh,
    they pop open at the other end. Or if he holds
       both ends, the middle splits—

and there's no stopping the steady migration
of the butterflies from his innards
out into the pasture . . .
Springing awake, he rises without any pause
from bed to his easle, and paints

his own figure leaning against the black
sage tree's trunk, while a spiralling long chain
of butterflies winds around man and tree
circling upwards, twenty-two in number as in his dream,
ranging
in size from tiny moth shapes near the man's
waist to great Monarch
butterflies large as swallows, gliding high
into uppermost branches. All colors
of Winfred's personality
group and regroup in the rainbow palette
of wing patterns, no two alike . . .

It rained all night. By daybreak, the sun
peeked between storm banks of cloud, and Winfred
plunged into a second tree canvas, an exercize
in perspective. A tall man, at far left, studies the black sage
tree across the meadow. Day overcast. Storm
thunderheads spreading
ever the middle upper rim. Brain rays are lines
diverging from his eyes to the tree's
widely branching puffed-out
top. A deluge of light—as if sourceless—comes
roaring out from behind the tree

like waves of a flash flood, spewn forth
        from an unseen backdrop. But waves of light—not
water—engulf the trunk and lower limbs, so
    blindingly sharp despite the tree's blocking any direct view
    of the original beams, the man must squint
        and shade his eyes with
            hand visor cupped over his brow to survey
        the gleamy expanse. SALTA, this super-
            charged light is called.
                He'd heard old tales about its inundations
                from the family elders, but now

encounters it for the first time pristinely.
        He holds his stance, but shudders in place, rocking
with the heaves of brightness—a glare that whips
    the viewer in the cheeks and forehead, shakes him from the roots
    of his hair to the pads of his toes. He is tough,
        a strong bold witness.
            He looks back at the light, unflinching. Never
    averts his eyes. It is a glory to him
            to have come upon
                this fierce gush and dazzle, at last. This holy
                blaze! Famed light of his ancestors . . .

THE POET ON THE POEM

"Exodus of Butterflies"

Deadlines. The day I completed this poem, I was slated to read it at the sumptuous glass house, the Poetry Foundation in Chicago. I'd never been in the building before. It was spring 2013. Later that year the poem was published in the VALPARAISO POETRY REVIEW. In early 2014, I was alerted online to the reprinting of my poem from the VALPARAISO POETRY REVIEW for the launching of the new magazine of Poetry and Poetics, HARTSKILL REVIEW. They cited this piece as their idea of a "great and beautiful poem" (December 2013) and the editor who chose my poem wrote a lovely, brief commentary to complement the online presentation. Today rereading the poem, I recall my two-week visit to the island in the ABCs that would become my favorite. From the moment I flew there from Curacao, Bonaire was the magical place that gave me my lifelong lucky number of 22. The day I met my special friend Franz Booi, the two of us kept finding a random succession of 22s. It seemed as if that number was an elf that mischievously kept stalking us. The number seemed to have a life of its own. The number was most luminous when we first observed the painting by Winfred Dania of 22 butterflies streaming out of the belly of a man standing beside a lone tree in the desert.

Franz and I soon discovered we were both 55 that day in 1990, and when we parted after the two week visit, we agreed we must meet again when we would be 80 years old. This very year… My first hour in Bonaire. As I strolled about the marketplace, I felt haunted, as if I must be fated to meet the charming loose-jointed man with the wide-brimmed floppy hat. When he noticed I was carrying a copy of my book THE CREOLE MEPHISTOPHELES he greeted me and asked to see the book. Shortly after, he introduced me to 17-year-old Winfred Dania, whom I presumed was his son. Winfred, who was a deaf mute, had been jailed the year before for selling drugs. Franz paid a fee to spring him from prison and agreed to be his "Bondsman" and guide. Winfred was a gifted artist. He loved to make pencil drawings. Franz told me that he himself was gainfully employed as Director, and curator, of the Bonaire museum. Local folks often came to him to hear him eloquently recite all 33 great myths of this culture. And his protégé loved to make drawings to illustrate each of the tales. I offered to write poems about some of the myths, and at my request, the two men shared the myths and drawings with me. I jotted the stories with pencil in my notepad, and Winfred - who could only speak with pictures – drew 33 small line sketches for me. One of my instant favorites was the portrait of a man whose unzipped abdomen released a sinuously winding arc of 22 butterflies. Another drawing of a man who viewed black storms in the distance also caught my attention. My poem assays to embody both myths with images. It should be chanted aloud. A windy twilight would be the best backdrop to help us visualize the colorful flight of butterflies; a campfire of dying embers, the best site for a reading.

CRUSH INTO THESE BLAKK FEET

I.

Soaring at heart,
dream kin they may be—Akyem and Basquiat—
though the pair never met: Ras Akyem's *ALTAR* both
Requiem for the Dead
and post-mortem revival of the Black
Haitian's sizzling raw art . . .
Three panels. A minimalist triptych
in black and white. Two finished versions. One, black-
on-white-backdrop, is the foremost.
The other (reduced
detail, more simplified), white-on-black. *See*
both. Keep looking at one, the other,
checking it out
feeling your way—
a bridge between them. For one may turn
the other inside out, as an X-ray reverses
our human body,
revealing to the doctor's eye strange
truth of hidden parts.
Black/White inversion—a comment on Race
(false dominances: who is on top, who now on bottom?)—
cannot be lost on the looker . . .
The three tall panels
are thickly white-oil-covered. They mimic
white walls of run-down city buildings
in slum backstreets

mostly ignored by police duos,
            where eye-scalding
graffiti spreads like wild ivy vines across
            sheets of stone. Bold
lettering travels at all angles,
            unstoppable: words often misspelled, or crossed-

            out and respelled
wrongly, some flickering with sparks
            of defiance, genius, gutter jokes, true pain or
            grief. Where they abound,
            urban sabotage reeks, for it stinks
of entrails, fish rot
            and gunpowder blent . . . Much white space
            in all three panels is crammed with those gray no-color
scrawls, word parts that appear grooved,
            dented or scraped
            into textured white ooze with the pointy back
end of paint brush. Black under-painting
            below the white
                        surface vaguely shows
            through, but blank white space still dominates . . .
            Cursory first glance at the tripartite work reveals
three black *SAMO* heads
                        upborne near the center of each paintscape.
            Those heads, like shaman
masks at Carnival, are death skulls. Squarish
            white eye-holes and sinister broad grins of white-toothed
            grillwork loom over those narrow
black jaws. Each death
            mask hovers in space, neckless, suspended
between two black columns of tombstone.
            With Matisselike

spare economy, those fewest black
lines and bars
hint a full monument propped over the still-open
grave in each trio
installment. They comprise a trinity
that adds up to one altar: ghoulish faces bobbing

like exhumed mock-
skulls of the martyred hero; or risen
image of his undying soul-perhaps bidden, coaxed,
to ascension by the act
of drafting the art work: *MAGICIAN
GURU SHAMAN* listed
at lower right, alongside that last
tomb column, exhales overtones of necromancy, witchcraft,
from the trancelike cast of square eyes
aglow in those dream-
stark heads. They could be paleolithic faces
lifted intact from cave walls . . .
The altar piece
speaks to us, mostly,
in top-to-bottom sweeps. But each mask, becapped
with its floating halo or *KROWN* of thorns, shimmers
over those tombside
fragments which, in left-to-right progression
across the three panel
units, come to resemble—more and more—

a human frame: from hips to ankles! And these secondary
horizontal readings of triptych
are adroitly prompted
by a few crossover graffiti that span,
or overlap, the hinges between panels:
CRUSH INTO THESE

BLAKK FEET, followed by the form
of actual man foot
in the L-shaped bottom of third left tombside,
mimicing the colossal
Stone-Foot-Of-Ramses. Man and monument
blent into a hybrid form at last, the whole series

building toward
this magical fusion—*hints of Basquiat's
Resurrection flashing here* . . . Two pairs of long
sinuous black bones
round out the scattered black patches
(oblongs, strips, and glary-eyed
Jack-o'-lanterns), spaced over pervasive
white oil portraiture. And *SPARE PARTS* is deeply
etched
above that far left bone set, as if
to say: stray dugup
bones of Basquiat's skeleton—femurs, upperleg
thigh bones they may be—are kept
in stock, salvaged
and at the ready
for use in art, like so many surplus car parts
stored up for repairs. Ras Akyem plies an old bone
kit for refashioning
broken lineaments of the honored dead—
his precursors, ancient
or modern . . . This fantasia compiles graphic
bio of the dead painter, rages to sum up his life story
and art with bare minimal images
or least word scraps.
The more random or accidental they look,
the more those hidden intensities shall
come streaking out . . .

Quite a plunge Ras takes into risky
format—his prior
best works aswirl with rich diversity of colors,
and crammed with a full
mosaic of textured detail. What cost
of Spirit to opt for wide sweeps of blanket WHITE.

WORDS ARE STONES. Graffiti words keep filling the gaps and voids,
blanks, negative space. More
       and more, scrawled words must carry
the missing weight—
paint mass of former blocks of color. The few streaks
             of tint, bold hue, flare out
starkly, and hurl a challenge at the black-on-white field
that would drive the color items away
    or send them diving down below white surface.
    Under-layers of orange, green, red
keep peeping out,

here & there. Blunt naked colors may weigh like tarnish on young
          black martyr's spirit, glares
     of disrespect for the dead. Mostly,
          Ras Akyem carries
    that full burden to express multitudes in Blacks & Whites . . .
        Perhaps three discrete sets
of offerings hang suspended, afloat, over each fractured
       silhouette of black altar and tomb frame.
      One little cluster of magic words and fine-line
       amulets, per panel. Each set hovers
         as if supported

on some invisible altar top: dream platter, shelflike, of unseen
hands. Offerings are held aloft,
    so many rich libations to be poured
for that teeming
Spirit . . . LEFT PANEL. The altar top presents a chess-board

pattern of crisscrossing
lines, not unlike smaller line-mesh that mimes a wide grimace
of teeth in the *SAMO* skulls poised up high.
    Two chess pieces—knight & king—appear: perhaps
    Basquiat's knight has already trounced
cocksure White King

since knight is propped squarely on board, king shoved offsides
           to the left. The Haitian artist
      had won his end-game with America, just
           before heroin
overdose took him! That chess match replays his streetsmart
      agile moves to outwit
most art dealers and gallery bosses in his New York heyday . . .
      MIDDLE PANEL. Five-petaled red flower,
pinwheel-shaped, lolls on its stem. Happy blossom
   · of the Resurrection, it strongly hints
        all *SAMO* heads—

transfixed above—be true ascendant face of the noble dead man.
VOODOO printed to the flower's
      right, an arrow below points across
black altar column
to A.D., orange under-coat showing through the white.
      These alphabets glimmer with
sparkles of some formula for raising the dead by Haitian
witchcraft, and bespeak promise of a saving
    afterlife for the martyred Ikon. Eerie nostalgias
    ripple back to childhood in his homeland . . .
Follow the arrow

across the panel break. Settle on that simplistic boat. Its one-
masted mini-sail puffed out
over a dugout shape seems to recall
old papyrus boats
sashaying down the Nile, slave ships of Middle Passage,
and those exile vessels
carrying Haitian boat people to America. *TO EAST* inscribed
above the tiny hull—sail back to your roots?
This transport craft, in turn, beckons overhead
to little red car shaped like a child's
toy auto labeled

TIN, taking us full-throttle forward to our modern day. A vision
that sweeps with ease and grace
from ancient Egypt and the African
Diaspora to both
artists' present moment: subject and maker of triptych . . .
RIGHT PANEL. Moving clockwise
from lower left, a card-deck Black Spade X'd out like some
word blocks. (Don't be fooled. Even Basquiat
confessed he often drew Xs or barred lines over
graffiti words to catch more notice—
never to delete,

cancel out, or correct, as a grammarian might.) That gamy spade
links up with the chess-board's
vanquished king, the spirit of gamesman-
ship a key motif
of both painters. Above the spade's inverted heartshape,
note a list of racial slur
words, common street epithets: *SPADE NEGROW NIGGA*
BLAKK

A couple are crossed out, as if street thug
is trying to choose among them—checking them
off, one by one, to get it just right
for this occasion.

Alongside the list, find two dangled fishhooks atilt like lures
to catch some passing feeder,
completing the contents of altar three.
Copyright logo,
appended over the hooks, a most telling clue: our painter,
himself, now claims all rights
of purchase. The viewer who nips the hooks and takes the bait,
as one who thinks he knows the true social
heft—or racial bite—of slur words, shall be fooled.
Snared like a caught fish! By image power,
Akyem reowns them

for his key design and art mission. Language, that double-edged
sword, is twisted. The words
lose their sting, taking on positive
nuance—epithet
or smudge now worn like badge of honor. Words of demeaning
poison become war cries
to silence the abusers . . . A black square frame surrounds *TAR*
within the word *ALTAR* of the painting's
title—center panel, bottom. And smears of black,
cagily faking sloppy or careless craft,
run like nosebleed

from the *TAR*-block down, as if dripping quick off canvas bottom,
exposing bright under-paint
            flecks of green. Streaks of whole color leap
out at the eye—
like random ink blots spattered on white backdrop. They steer
                    the inquiring beholder's
search for meaning, answers to those riddles set in motion
by leading players in the picture bio . . .
        A gold-orange trio, running from diagonal corner
        to corner across the whole three-part
expanse, discloses

quiet personal message, or secret confession, from yours truly—
                    architect of the altar. Gold-
            tinged mushrooms, below the Rastafarian's
                    witch-doctor list,
        reveal his own leaning to hallucinogens, his debt to mind
            expanders, a fraternal link
        to his sadly *O-DEED* model. The diagonal gold sweep runs
            through red-orange *TIN* car in mid-panel
        upon the small gold crown, upper left, perhaps
            reserved for his humble aspiring self,
                    a would-be Knight

following in his mentor's art glory path. If that slanted chain
of faint gold figures belongs
        to Akyem's own private history, unfolding
here in Barbados
today, a mystery triangle of red emblems near the work's
                    center—like the Bermuda
Triangle at sea—may decode other puzzle parts. The red smear
under-named *SCAR*, its low point. High point,
        one large red crown, above-named *KING PLEASURE.*

And the aforementioned five-petaled
red flower forms

isosceles mid-point. While *SCAR* gash marks out pains and wounds
        of Basquiat's early dying,
    flower and *KROWN*—taken together—radiate
        hope of afterlife
sainthood. Or Kingly Resurrection. Altar piece is moulded,
      then, both as elegy
tribute, and as maker Akyem's sacerdotal shaping of his three-
      paneled Miracle. He would offer up
  his paint flesh as ransom, placed on the altar
    shelf of God's hand—to insure second
        life for Basquiat.

(after the painting "Altar for Jean-Michel Basquiat,"
by Ras Akyem, 1995)

Acknowledgments

The author gratefully acknowledges the following journals in which these poems originally appeared:

American Poetry Review:	"The Pope In St. Lucia (parts 1, 5, 16)
	"The Poet On the Poem"
	"White Gold"
	"Humpback, Through a Spyglass"
Colorado Review:	"House of Bone Chandeliers"
Fifth Wednesday Journal:	"Chagall's Rabbi: Black Fire On White Fire"
	"Undying Is An Art: Song of Captain Hodge"
	"Opera"
Five Points:	"Relics of the Bonfire"
	"Largesse"
Hudson Review:	"Granddad and the Humpbacks"
Kenyon Review:	"Crush Into These Blakk Feet"
The New Yorker:	"Transvestite"
Poetry Daily:	"White Gold"
	"Relics of the Bonfire"
Shenandoah:	"Angel's Jawbone"
Southwest Review:	"Divemaster: Swimming With the Immortals"
Valparaiso Poetry Review:	"Exodus of Butterflies"
The Cummington Press:	"The St. Kitts Monkey Feuds"

BOOKS BY LAURENCE LIEBERMAN

POETRY

Hour of the Mango Black Moon (2004)

Flight From the Mother Stone (2000)

The Regatta in the Skies: Selected Long Poems (1999)

Compass of the Dying (1998)

Dark Songs: Slave House and Synagogue (1996)

The St. Kitts Monkey Feuds (1995)

New and Selected Poems: 1962–92 (1993)

The Creole Mephistopheles (1989)

The Mural of Wakeful Sleep (1985)

Eros at the World Kite Pageant (1983)

God's Measurements (1980)

The Osprey Suicides (1973)

The Unblinding (1968)

CRITICISM

Beyond the Muse of Memory: Essays On Contemporary American Poets (1995)

Unassigned Frequencies: American Poetry in Review (1977)

The Achievement of James Dickey (1968)